# ANCHOR BOOKS

THE LOVE WITHIN US

Edited by

Heather Killingray

First published in Great Britain in 1997 by
ANCHOR BOOKS
1-2 Wainman Road, Woodston,
Peterborough, PE2 7BU
Telephone (01733) 230761

HB ISBN 1 85930 536 9
SB ISBN 1 85930 531 8

FOREWORD

Anchor Books is a small press, established in 1992, with the aim of promoting readable poetry to as wide an audience as possible.

We hope to establish an outlet for writers of poetry who may have struggled to see their work in print.

The poems presented here have been selected from many entries. Editing proved to be a difficult task and as the Editor, the final selection was mine.

This is a delightful collection of poems written by people who have experienced love in their life, whether it be love for a relative, friend or lover. All are sharing with us their strongest emotions within this anthology.

The poems in this book have been selected because they communicate with the reader. The poets express their thoughts and feelings for someone close to them, whether it be admiration, respect or love. All this can be found throughout this collection.

I trust this selection will delight and please the authors and all those who enjoy reading poetry.

Heather Killingray
Editor

CONTENTS

MISSING YOU

My darling man I loved you so
I wonder why you had to go
I did not want you to stay in pain
Now only my broken heart remain

I try to be brave and face life now
But I'm only a lonely woman somehow
As I sit by the fire I feel you near
And it's only a stupid dream I fear

Remember the day I became your bride
We came from the church side by side
I felt in a trance and did not see
The people there who looked at me

But it's all gone now though I'm still the bride
But with never the bridegroom by my side

Never to hear your voice again
Never to hold your hand
Never to lie in your arms again
Seems more than I can stand

Lonely without you both night and day
My heart beating but in vain
Calling your name over again
Loving you just the same

Now I live in a dream love
With a heart that's broken inside
There's so much pain caring in vain
This is my life without you

Edith Gash

TOUCHING

I touch you in the beauty
of your sleep
I touch you in the treasured
memories I keep
I touch your lips so perfect
so sweet
I touch your hand your eyes
when we meet
I touch you in the wonder
of our love
I touch you tho' you are in
the heavens above
And all of this touching in my
memories of pride
Will always be with me till I'm
again by your side.

J Daddy

BURNING

Over and over
I re-read your lines,
walls growing darker
the fire still alight
and a clock
to mark the dead hour.

TV stands silent
alone with the dust,
I retread the carpet
your voice at my ear
in a room that
never let go

This is a bottle
and this a gloved hand,
music to dance
and singing out loud:
instructions
to lock the last door.

John Steer

No Through Road

Ever been caught in an emotional cul-de-sac
And wondered how you came there?

The avenue was tree-lined,
The verge was lush and green,
The route ahead looked promising:
The pavement bore a sheen.

The way mapped out before us,
Time passing gave no worry:
Streets were made for meandering
And we were in no hurry.

But now I'm lost in a dead-end road -
No traffic passes through;
And leaf gives way to litter
With time I've wasted on you.

The vows they lie in pieces,
The dress and veil hang torn,
And the future persists
Like a cold grey mist
That hails the coming dawn.

Jean Price

THE PURPLE DOOR

as she came through the door
looking rather tired
he said:
forgotten to buy a loaf again, haven't yer?
i'm sick of it , i really am
so am i, she said

both were furious

could have bought one, you know
had plenty of time, all day
not on your life, he said
want to know, what they are saying, do yer?
here it comes:
married to that big foreign one
hasn't he changed since he's got married?
she's got him well under the thumb
i'm telling yer now
and you'd better get it straight
i'm not buying no loaves, and that's that

she didn't answer this time
no luck again at the labour exchange, she thought
and stormed into the small back-kitchen, ready to attack
the dirty dishes
but there wasn't a dish to be seen
not one, and
he had painted the door
an awful purple colour

he had followed her
what yer think? lovely, eh?
a mate give me the paint
fell of the back of a lorry, i suppose

she burst out laughing
he just stood there
looking at her
not knowing what to think

she laughed until
at last
he joined in
then she went over to him
gave him a big kiss and said:
purple, eh?
my favourite colour
must have taken you all day

Alfa

YOU STEPPED FROM MY DREAMS

I loved you from the first moment I ever saw you.
All I did was look at you and I knew,
For I felt magic deep inside I'd never ever felt before,
Couldn't believe I'd met you at last, with
                    every moment I wanted you more.
I'd only met you in my dreams you were always at my side,
But when I awoke each morning I only had thoughts and cried,
Now my dreams have come alive, it's hard to believe that it's true.
Now I can hold you and kiss you, and really know that it's you.
It's not dreams I want they are no good it
                    has to be the real thing for me,
You stepped from my dreams into my life, and
                    together we will always be.

Linda Roberts

THE THRILL OF THE CHASE

I thought at first
My task in vain,
But with wiles
And giles
A few white lies,
Eventually
I got a date.

Is she aware
Of my stare?
Thigh length boots
On high bar stool
Long slim legs,
Can't help
But drool!

Candle-lit dinners
In small Greek places,
A bit of sporting
On the beaches,
Devious courting,
Lovely features.

Kept her photo in my pocket
And swaggered round
And showed it,
Proud as punch
Sometimes drunk,
I hardly could
Believe it.

After a while
It seemed the time
We had so much in common,
I wish I knew
What she'd do
If I popped the question.

Heart thumping
Adrenaline running
Trying
Not to show it.

Now's the time
It's do or die
Lucky
She said 'yes'.

David Madeira-Cole

JUST A CERTAIN FEELING

What is love, can it be analysed?
I have come to realise
That I don't know why
This glow inside me,
That makes me view the world,
As a jewel, gleaming bright.
So very new to this poor fool
Who wants to give her heart
To that special one who will plead:
'Please be mine,
I really need and love you all the time!'
Why do I feel this way?
That joy has really come to stay.
And life is a pleasure
Just to think of him,
Is a thrill to treasure,
I no longer have to fill my leisure
With hopes and fears,
This thing called love
Is sure to last all my years.

Freda Tester-Ellis

PAST LOVE

There is an unknown man that once I loved,
Not of this world nor even p'raps the next,
But in some dim distant past we loved.
I saw a photograph of him once,
Immediately I knew he was the one
And we had loved beyond all boundaries.
It was not you, nor you, or even you.
I thought I loved you once, or you, or you,
But when I saw that photograph I knew
It was not true, this man was part of me.
I cannot have that faded photograph
Of a girl's grandfather when he was young,
How could I explain to her I knew him?
But it is certain that some time ago
We were lovers once, a long time past.

Valerie Conway

A PARTING PRAYER

Wherever we go
however far
home is always where you are
won't you leave the door ajar
for me to enter there

and when we must
be far apart
I, in the garden of my heart
feel the growth of longing start
and tend it with a prayer.

Sara Russell

FROM A FLANDERS FIELD

My dearest May, I miss you
So much, why are we apart?
This war is mad, is stupid,
Why did it have to start?

Only thoughts of you my dear,
Your gentleness, your love,
Can be my shield, my armour,
As death rains down from above.

In filthy trench I sit alone,
And traverse memory lane,
I feel your hand caress my cheek,
Hear your sweet voice again.

I know my days are numbered,
In this imperfect life,
So keep these thoughts forever,
My love, my darling wife.

Inas Everett

FEELINGS

The colour of true love,
Is very rarely seen,
The feeling of true love,
Has always always been,
The secret of true love,
To find and both to share,
The pleasure of true love,
To please, and both must care,
To love and to be loved,
Is equally enjoyed.

Elizabeth Lee

LOST LOVE

You were my joy,
my heaven, my bliss.
Even now, I am
thankful for this.

It was magic for me,
each time that we met.
When I could hold thee,
my eyes were all wet.

Tears for the future?
Then I knew not,
that time would untie
our true lover's knot.

When I could love thee,
my eyes were all bright.
Full of thy beauty,
from morn until night.

Now that I lost thee
were thou ever so dear.
How did I lose thee?
By jealousy and fear.

Peter Sowter

CONSTANCY

Love is constant, lasting, true,
And will not be denied.
No need ever to renew
That truly special kind.

Love where hearts are intertwined
And none will say, 'I've won.'
So unlike a love beguiled
Where selfish deeds are done.

Recall sometimes is delayed
But deep within our sighs
Loving memories never fade,
No real love . . . ever dies.

Grace Leeder-Jackson

TOGETHER

When first we two became one,
We squandered our days -
Happy whether on heights,
Or life's occasional valleys . . .
So long as we were together.
Then our one acquired another three,
And love had to expand;
Sometimes to be bruised,
But essentially always to stand firm.
When the three in turn became a one,
Love's bounds stretched even wider.
Now we look on their young,
Marvelling at their nonchalance
Controlling strange knobs speaking a Lingua Technic.
Time is suddenly flying by,
We plan in weeks not years:
A touch, the face in a room
Become ever more important.
Some day we know there will only be half of one,
Yet through the tears
There will remain our hoarded treasures . . .
A place, a voice, a joke
For ever held in memory,
Of a love constant and strong,
Binding, but always free.

Di Bagshawe

IF ONLY

If only we'd taken the time to cry
If only we'd reason or wonder why
If only we'd stumbled or fallen short
If only we'd kissed and not been caught
If only this was our romance
If only we had just one more chance

If only we'd taken the time to see
If only we'd had the chance to be
If only I'd held you one more time
If only love was not a crime
If only this was sweet romance
If only I'd not spoilt my chance

If only I'd not laid down the law
If only I'd not become a bore
If only your eyes would sparkle and shine
If only your heart was mine, all mine
If only you'd see how much I care
If only I'd wake and find you there

Lee James Nelson

EMOTIONS

From my heart these emotions flow
I'm bursting with love and it will grow
Cupid's arrows have pierced my heart deep
My dreams are disturbed and I cannot sleep
So hurry my love to my side
For my feelings for you I cannot hide,
Our hearts will be entwined forever,
My love for you will leave me never.

D Mellors

FIRST ANNIVERSARY

With this verse, I mark the formal distance
That has now been reached, in both of our lives,
Simultaneously, but not by chance,
Since this day has been cut by the long knives,
Notching up three hundred and sixty-five days:
One whole year; a solemn landmark indeed.
And, looking back, there are so many ways
In which I wish that things could have been changed.
Change - that perennial wish. But, it's true,
One thing that I would in no manner change,
And that is this year that I've spent with you:
Every moment so right, so unstrange.
Our second year is now ready to start,
Take with it my dreams, and all of my heart.

Chris Moores

COULD I BUT LOVE YOU

Could I but love you for yourself awhile,
Could I forget the magic of your eyes,
Your hair, your cheeks, your lips, your hands, your smile -
Then could I still discordant doubts that rise
Like laughter o'er the music of my love:
      'When these are gone, when youthful lustre fades
      The bloom is vanished and the glory passed,
      And time has dulled the dainty pastel shades
      And age advances oh so fast, so fast,
      Will you still love her?' And I say 'My love
      Is for herself, not for her mortal wealth.'
My heart, however, knows these words for lies:
There were some hope that I could love you for yourself,
Could I forget the magic of your eyes.

Peter Fenwick

THOMAS LUKE

Ten days early, not waiting until the date
no time for hospital, a home birth was our fate
labour endured with the help of gas and air
husband and wife, an experience for us to share
April 25th, hands on the clock tick slowly past noon
a gathered hush descends, the time is soon
broken by the cries and urges of midwife and mother
tiny head emerging, for Samuel Connor a little brother
Thomas Luke born wide-eyed into the waking world
perfect toes and fingers wrinkled, tightly curled
raindrops spatter on wet paving outside the room
a shaft of light breaks through the gathering gloom
baby's cry brings forth fresh comfort and joy
Linda and Ruth deliver to Julie a beautiful boy
proud Nanna was witness, cutting the cord
another new voice that cannot be ignored
passed to the happy father beaming face alight
cuddled bundle of blankets a wonderful sight
weighing in at 6lb 10oz a bouncing healthy son
a safe arrival for all concerned, now begins the fun

Paul Birkitt

MISSING YOU

I only miss you
When the wheatfields grow
When the evening comes
When the rivers flow

I only miss you
When the hawthorn's in bloom
When the autumn comes
In this lonely room

I only miss you
When the lambkins play
On a springtime day
I only miss you
Each and every day

Michael Wixon

COME LOVE

Come love come spring come daffodils
To fill the empty heart
When all the seasons turn away
Love still will not depart.
Because I did not look for love
Love came and looked for me.
Because I did not speak to love
Love spoke . . . incessantly
And followed me both day and night
And would not let me be.
Love called to me in the scented air
Along the bluebell way
Across the wind did call to me
Did call, and bid me stay,
With voice as soft as morning dew
And warm as a young spring breeze
That creeps away from the winter chills
To turn life's patient pace around
With her bursting daffodils.
Come love and cast your magic thrills
Come flowers thick upon the hills,
Come spring let bluebells scent the way
Through every shady lane,
Love called to me in the perfumed air
Love called me, and I came.

Constance Ivy Roper

MY WORLD

All that I love in this world is here,
　　Under one roof, beside my fire:
Everything I need -
　　　　Comfort and beautiful memories
All I long for -
　　　　All I desire.

A kind dear home, that shelters me,
　　With its tender hand,
　　　　　　Upon the door.
For - if the least harm befalls,
　　　　There will be,
Never a home,
　　　　To hold me anymore.

A kindly thatch, overhead,
　　And the snug warmth of a cosy bed:
And as I rise,
　　　　In my own special way,
I say -
　　　　Thank You Lord,
　　　　　　for this new day.

Irene Hurd

MY LOVE

When I tak' your haun' in mine
An' gaze deep intae your eyes
I see the lovelicht shine
Like the sun in tropic skies.
As oor tremmlin' fingers twine
Tae draw you close tae me
I ken your love is mine
An' forever mair will be.

Oh! Had I the siller tongue
Or the gift o' poesie,
The sweetest sang that's sung
Couldnae tell my love o' thee.
While the moon, in the Heavens hung,
An' the staurs eternal shine,
Till the last death knell is rung,
Ma hert is ayeways thine.

John Millar

WAITING

The days are long
The nights so drear
When you my love
Are far from here.
I count the hours
Until you come
But until then
My heart is numb.
I fill each day
With work and things
And watch the 'phone
Until it rings.
And when you call
Your voice I hear
And all is well
You seem so near.
But best of all
Is when we meet
For every hour
With you is sweet.

Sheila Phelan

NOT KNOWING

If you were coming in a month,
I'd count the days with care;
But never for a moment once
Doubt that you'd be here.

If I could see you in the spring
I'd laugh the winter through
And mock the icicles that cling
To tears I've shed for you.

If you were coming in a year
The months could be denied
Until, at once, you would appear
And never leave my side.

If I could say that this decade
You'd come and comfort me
I would not feel so half afraid
That it will never be.

Not knowing when it is you'll come,
Each second seems a year,
Each minute a millennium
Of grief and hope and fear.

Campbell Kay

KEN

So much love in the morning
Being two but feeling as one
Your head on my pillow
My heart in your hand
A new life together
In our magic land

Hev Woodhouse

LOVE

The roses he sends me are red
Their perfume goes straight to my head
He's always loving, tender and kind
Each kiss from him just blows my mind
He sets my body on fire
He fills me with such desire
I am happy just being in his arms
He fills me with his tender charms
I love him with my body and my soul
His love makes me feel complete and whole
I've been with him for thirty years
We have shared happiness, heartaches and fears
My hope now is that day by day
As we walk life's narrow way
That we shall love each other
Be faithful and true to one another
Until the final day comes to part
Breaking forever the strings of my heart.

Rachel Jarvis

LOVE LIES NEXT TO ME

Awash with almost sleep
Swamped by the darkness of total night
Listening to the buzz of silence
I anticipate the delicious taste of slumber
Contemplating the ways of man
Marvelling the wonder of love
How it lies somewhere between eloquence and elegance
How love lies next to me.

Dave Lunn

CUPIDITY

I said goodbye to romance
When I said goodbye to you,
I said goodbye forever, to a dream
That couldn't come true.
Chance dictated our meeting,
And fate decided we part,
But as my fondest memory,
You stay within my heart.

How can I forget you?
When each and every day,
This melancholia plays a tune
That will not fade away.

Is anyone that trusts in Cupid,
Simply being - just plain stupid?

Sam Stafford

SHE GAVE ME, LONG AGO

I remember, as a child, she sat me on her knee,
Though busy with her daily chores, she found the time for me.
Her tired worn hands stroked tenderly, to soothe away my tears,
And when in doubt, her guiding hand, would banish all my fears.
Within my dreams, I see her now, her gentle touch to guide,
I never knew how much she gave, until I left her side.
Now she's gone, I wish her near, to hold my hand when sad,
To comfort me when I feel lost, as when a little lad.
If only I had hugged her close, been good, when she was tired,
And treated her as she did me, with comfort if she cried.
An angel, sent from Heaven above, a boy too young to know,
May Heaven give her all the love, she gave me, long ago.

Thomas Victor Healey

OBSESSIVE LOVE

Should I live to be a hundred I could never find the time
to tell you all the reasons why I'm glad that you are mine.
I love to see you when the sun shines on your lovely face,
the smile you give to greet me, your warm, tender embrace.
The way your eyes search round for me across a crowded room,
the trembling in my foolish heart as I smell your faint perfume.
I find you so appealing with a smudge upon your nose
or when you're quietly writing with your peaceful, gentle pose.
I love your great excitement when you find a new bird's nest,
but most of all I love you when my head rests on your breast.
I love you more with each new day, with every breath I take.
If ever you should leave me I'd no more want to wake
for life would hold no worth for me.
I would leave this earth and set you free.

Helen Strangwige

LOVE OF MINE

Love of mine, what are you to me?
Look into my heart and you will see,
I'm so proud to share your name,
To be touched by your kisses sweet as rain,
You are my joy, my love for life,
I'm a well contented, happy wife,
Look even deeper if you can,
My ever-loving, faithful man,
To see, my love, a burning ember,
As our wedding day, I remember,
Now twenty-five years gone in the past,
Our wonderful love it will last and last,
Last, throughout all eternity,
You are this precious, my love to me.

L P Smith-Warren

KISS FROM A STAR

Your love gives richness
of countless wealth.
It is more precious than
breath itself.

The meaning of my life
the reasons for me.
A great strength in your softness
for the world to see.

Your warmth is wafted
on angels' wings.
It gives me faith
in so many things.

My comfort in pillows
sweet dreams you send.
A kiss from a star
at the rainbow's end.

Dewi Wyn Hughes

LOVE

Many years have gone by
When I fell in love
American he was
Which I loved
But to war he went
And left me behind
He got killed on the line
With all the others.
The love is still there
But I think of others.

Lilian Coombs

DO YOU LOVE ME

(For Jock and Debra)

Do you love me
Like I love you
As the sun loves the day
As the day loves the dawn
As the dawn loves the song
Of the birds.

Do you love me
Like I love you
As the wind loves the cloud
As the cloud loves the rain
As the rain loves the fall
From the sky.

Do you love me
Like I love you
As the leaf loves the tree
As the tree loves the earth
As the earth knows its worth
I know I love you.

And at the end of my years
When my days have turned to prayers
I know I'll have just one thing left to say
Do you love me
Like I love you

John Forest Gaunt

I'M HERE FOR YOU NOW

I'm here for you now
As always I've been
Through thick and through thin
With no in-between
And time will be endless
For just you and I
So many tomorrows
And never goodbye.

I'm here for you now
And want you to know
That I will be with you
Wherever you go
So smile and be happy
And live for today
And know that, my darling,
I'm yours come what may.

Shirley Whiles

ALWAYS

The laughter in your bright eyes,
Sometimes falls on me,
The sadness in your mind's eye,
Still wishing it was free,
My lady with your burden,
Laying heavy on your heart,
Move close and hold me tightly,
And we'll let the healing start,
I don't know your inner feelings,
But be sure, one thing is true,
Whichever way your heart goes,
This man's still loving you.

J C Boxall

YOU'VE GOT ME WHERE YOU WANT ME

Within our silence,
hear the sound of love.
Eyes are windows,
windows of the soul;
true love is more,
more precious than gold.
Silence is talking,
hear its words of love.

I love you with every part
of my body, every part,
and you are every breath I breathe.
My idea of Hell on Earth
would be to live without you;
life would be worthless should you leave.

Love you with my mind and soul,
I love you absolutely,
you are my reason to exist.
For you there is not a thing
I wouldn't do, not a thing,
there's not a chance I could resist.

You've got me where you want me
and I'm happy to be there,
all the day, heart's on fire,
all the night, love's desire.
You've got me where you want me
and I'm happy to be there,
drowning in ecstasy,
your love means all to me.
You've got me where you want me
and I'm happy to be there.

Pauline Ilsley

FOR MY HUSBAND

Love is someone who cares when you're sad
Love is someone who's pleased when you're glad
Love is someone you want to be near
Love is someone who takes away fear
Love is snuggling close up to at night
Love is making just everything right
Love is sadness when we are apart
Love is arms that hold me to your heart
Love is laughter and days full of fun
Love is tender and feelings as one
Love is special with feelings so true
Love is sacred and someone like you.

Sandra Farmer

TO ANNETTE

What can I offer thee Annette but love?
My inspiration, and all else above:
All the known laws of nature I have plied;
Each various grace and virtue I have tried:
Been kind and cruel, generous and mean,
That I may win a place in thy esteem:
My only fault, if any fault it be;
My only crime, it is in loving thee:
And yet just now, you glory in your youth,
Fly from fond love disdaining; but in truth,
If we may not our different natures blend;
At least let's share the pleasures of a friend:
For, better to have seen the moon's pale light,
Than walk forever in eternal night.

Alexander K Sampson

SUCH LOVE - SO PURE

Lift high your lament unto spreading hills,
      O heart which swoons in bliss,
for all creation shall share your thrills,
      amid rapture's sweet tender kiss.

Such ecstasy embrace my flustered brow,
      amid tranquillity grant your stay,
thus, eternal fulfilment be thy vow,
      'tween true loves upon springtime's day.

O stem of life to thee I plead
      touch not two hearts with dread.
As we sow now love's garden seed,
      grant prosperity's grace instead.

Such love - so pure, now conquer to last.
      With solace to embrace our days,
then, with my true love shall we cast
      all solemn beyond vanquished ways.

S Kettlewell

JUST

Just to feel your arms around me
Just to feel you hold me tight
Just to know you're there beside me
In the middle of the night
Just to wake up with the knowledge
You'll be there all day for me
Makes the next few days worth living
Turns the 'you' and 'I' to 'we'.

Gwynn Watt

A CRY FROM THE HEART

I pen this poem my loved one
To tell you just how I feel,
Oh I my darling miss you
My true love I now reveal.

I think about the good times
That I know we surely had
Why then did you desert me
Leaving me alone, and sad.

I will not e'er forget you
How you wooed me night and day
What went wrong and why you left
Well I really cannot say.

I know there is no other
Who will ever take your place,
I have now just a memory
Of your happy smiling face.

Seems like only yesterday
On the days we used to meet,
With heart so light I floated
Down the street on winged feet.

I wish to hear you knocking
Once again on my front door,
Welcome you with open arms,
Please dear grant my wish once more.

And so my dearest loved one,
Heed these words and hear my plea,
Afore more time has passed by,
Oh, please, please return to me.

Barbara Sowden

LOVE TO DO WHAT'S RIGHT

Want to say yes:
love to say no.

Want to tell a lie:
love to tell the truth.

Want to be cross:
love to keep calm.

Want to give up:
love to persevere.

Want to sit down:
love to walk a mile.

Want to steal the limelight:
love to stay in the wings.

Neville Hawkins

HILL-TOP SONG

Once you said that I was all your world
As we stood together on a windy hill.
The fleecy clouds of sunset pearled
And a bird retiring gave a happy trill.
But since that evening when we both stood there,
I with a new song in my heart
You with the breeze on your dark hair,
A little frost with cruel icy fingers
Has touched us both, and left us so alone.
But down the passage of the years I will remember
Because my hill-top song into true love has grown

Hilda M Evans

A DREAM ABOUT FLO

I dreamt you held your heart above
Your head and demonstrated love
By casting it into the air
Above a tranquil lakelet, where
I heard it pierce the water still,
Thus causing it with waves to fill,
Which outward in their circles went,
Thus by your heart on errand sent
O'er all the lake that is my world:
As happy peace those ripples swirled,
For what on my life's lake . . . apart
From that . . . could issue from your heart?

Peter S A Cooper

WHAT IS LOVE?

A sea that stirs you from within
and sends your heart into a spin
a drum inside your ears will beat
and then come crashing at your feet
your temperature will start to rise
all is revealed through loving eyes
also the pain is most intense
it doesn't really make much sense
how can love make you feel so bad
instead of absolutely glad
but please do not despair my friend
this is by no means the end
all will be a bed of roses
when your dearest one proposes

Ann Boyd

THE BALANCE OF LOVE

'How much love today?
How little to weigh?' -
My heart is heavy
When you feel this way.

'Tomorrow is new,
Will my love come through?' -
Why do you question
And torture me too?

'Should my feelings fall,
My passion too small?' -
Have you really no faith
In your love at all?

'It's not love I fear -
Only liking you - near.'
You have only to call
When you want me dear.

I love you each day,
In all different ways.
I don't measure love -
Just give it and say

I'm here, just until
I'm not needed still.
So love me your way,
Just give as you will.

Not much at a time -
Or make my eyes shine.
Don't measure my heart -
Add your love to mine.

Julie Creaven

MOON DANCER

I saw her dancing
In the light
Clouds were drifting
Through the night
I did not even know her name
But from that point
My life
Would never be the same.
I reached out to touch her
To let her know I care
When I did she disappeared
And then she was not there
Clouds by now were
Covering over the moon
Breathing a sigh
Saying goodbye
It all had ended much too soon.
Now she's gone
Life goes on
Memories of what could have been.
I will always remember
The picture of beauty
That I was lucky to have seen.

George Glen

TOGETHER

Two lovers together starting off today
Scared of the future, scared of what to say
They've got a lifetime together to sort things out
So forget the past, it's the future that counts.

Each day should be filled with laughter and care
Helping each other, just being a pair
They have an aim in life now
A challenge it must be worthwhile
Two people together learning to smile.

Jean Ruddy

FOREVER

Every touch, every smell, every taste
Every word, every vow, all gone to waste

Every hope, every dream, every life
Every joy, every mood, were crushed inside

Every scene, every laugh, every tear
Every dawn, every night, now laced with fear

Every beat, every hour, every day
Every pulse, every nerve, slowly fade away

Every inch, every yard, every mile
Every bruise, every scar, can't raise a smile

Every now, every then, every sigh
Every loss, every pain, why bother to try?

Every smile, every face, everyone
Every place, everywhere, but you are gone

Every road, every plan, every choice
Every breath, every silence, never your voice

Forever yours
Forever . . .

Bernard Harry Reay

HARD TO RESIST

Granite heart? Huh! Tempted by the taste
All around. Breathe the utter waste.
Money changing hands. Bread for some poor kids?
Blustering betting men - Mikes and Freds and Sids
Lust for better things for their kith and kin
Instead they might as well chuck their money in the bin.
Now's the time to leave! Don't succumb! Please go!
Greyhounds, nags and pools made you lowest of the low.

Put those years behind you! You're a lucky man!
All your family stayed. For you a second chance.
Such compassion's rare when you lie and cheat.
So don't betray their trust. Don't start to retreat
Into former ways. Wife or lady luck? Now's the time to choose.
Once you've made your mind up one of them will lose.
Nervous palpitations, sweating, breathing fast.
Slam the door behind you! Love of gambling's in the past.

Angela Y Kerrin

OPEN HEART

I opened my heart and let you inside.
The way I was feeling left nowhere to hide.
I knew that the way I was feeling, for me was wrong,
But, when I was near you my heart sang a song.
It helped me to see that my heart had survived,
For two years ago I thought it had died.
Now, that 'my heart being open', has come to an end,
I hope you'll allow me, to still be your friend.

Alison Wood

ANSWERED PRAYERS

A shadow is seen sitting in the midnight hour,
    Holding a rose, which is now a dead flower.
He whispers a question so clearly,
    Waiting for an answer, so patiently.

Suddenly, he stands up to feel the rain pelting down,
    Then slips and hits his head on the ground.
His face is smudged from the mud on the floor,
    As he casts his memories, to the days in the war.

He shivers with cold and crawls into a ball,
    And thinks back to the days, when he had it all.
He was strong and always did fight,
    Never would give up, until he was right.

From the fall that he has had,
    He wants to die, he feels alone and sad.
He looks to the sky and says, 'Let me die,
    Please help me Lord,' he cried.

He turns his head, what does he see?
    His family looking at him helplessly.
He thinks he can live, is it too late?
    As he stretches his arms out straight.

His prayers were heard, his family came,
    Now he will not live, each day in pain.
He has his memories, which are his past,
    While he lives happily, with his dreams that will last.

Abida Haidar

SECRET RENDEZVOUS

Wait for me, beside the river
Birth a love for my coming
Embrace a crisp autumn dawn shiver
Absorb the songbird's gentle humming.

Travel with shadows, witness no soul
Disguise the path to our tryst
Flee the shackles of imperious control
Pursue the essence that you insist.

Hearts woven with intricate delicacy
A diamond web in frost
Fruits of a distant legacy
The emergence of a secret once lost.

Over there, beneath the arms of wilted willow
Consume the precious time we endure
Come, your love I shall pillow
And comfort our peace forever more.

Soloman Mohamed

HEARTACHE

I heard a whisper that you're coming home
I'm bewildered and numb from this sudden shock
This feeling inside me it's running wild
What will you say when you see me and my child?

Deny if you like the joys of fatherhood
I'll not pressure you to love my beautiful boy
Torment and insecurity were both thrust my way
When your ship left harbour a year ago today.

How I loved you the only man in my world
Breathless moments of lust our exotic love
Yet so far away, lost in time
Never to recapture the feelings of your warm embrace.

I heard a whisper that you bring a wife . . .
I'm a shadow lost on a rainy day
Frustration is tearing at my heart,
Though I look at my son, I know you're a part.

June Elizabeth Baden

THE FIRST TIME

Awaken to me
beautiful child,
let your spirit soar
and your heart run wild.
For I shall show you
a thousand things,
an eternal song
for your heart to sing.

Your innocent eyes
shall see a new,
no empty shell
of life for you.
All your tomorrows
I shall bring,
so feast on this night
of everything.

Paula Brown

LOVE THAT KNOWS NO BOUNDARIES

With all the golden moments and blessings that you share,
Two hearts are joined as one to show each other that you care.
May all the days ahead continue as the days now gone,
Those times of youthful happiness for all the years to come.

With such romantic notions to fill a maiden's head
And plans to make to share a life together as you'd said.
Exciting days you both would have with all the world to see,
They too would share the love and wonder of your majesty.

The time has passed but love has grown still steadfast in its way,
Whilst all the nation watches and thinks well of you today.
A special anniversary that's stood the test of time,
And all best wishes sent to you, some even in a rhyme.

That the highest high in all the land should fall to cupid's bow,
Inspires a hope in all of us; the lowest of the low.
That truest love will favour not no rank or station found,
Just heart's desire of all the hopes that deep within abound.

Beverley Hill

FIRST LOVE

With heart singing and bells ringing,
The sun brighter, footsteps lighter,
Oh! Happy day I'm on my way
To my true love.

Passion waking, overtaking
Every caution. Not a portion
Of such sweet bliss would I dare miss
Of this my love.

Love is living, love is giving,
Love is blooming, all consuming,
Each day filling, overspilling
With thoughts of you.

Jean M White

JIM

I love a man, his name is Jim
And I'll do anything for him.

I'll scrub his floors and cook his food,
And then he'll kiss me when I'm good.

I'll wash his clothes and darn his socks,
And run my fingers through his locks.

And after work, when he comes home,
I'll have his supper nice and warm.

And when day's done, two sleepy heads,
Will wander up the stairs to bed.

And in the quiet of the night,
I'll hug him hard, he'll hold me tight.

We'll kiss and love the whole night through,
A cosy nest for just we two.

And in the morning, when day breaks,
I'll softly kiss him wide awake.

And gently send him on his way,
For us, to start another day.

I love a man, his name is Jim,
And I am going to marry him!

Cynthia Morgan

TOGETHER

Though the months have gone
Last year's leaves still remain,
Huddling the ground where our footsteps trod,
A reminder of yesterdays,
That was the summer of our lives,
Now I walk the woods alone,
Talking as if you were there,
Holding on to memories
That crinkle fragile edge of crumbling leaf.

Dearest Jonathan, your presence sadly missed
With the exchange of tweed and flannel
For khaki green.
Sunburnt face lost its colour
Since you went away.

Snowdrops are now again in bloom my love,
I gathered them placed them on the alter,
With a prayer for you.
I do so hope before another spring to pass
You'll be by my side?

Primroses have come and gone
But still no sign of your return,
Till then, in melancholy mood,
I walk the woods alone -
Listening to the cuckoo calling
To bring you back to me,
Please make it soon before another summer's gone.

June days now have turned to autumn's fall,
Leaves tumble down to huddle the ground once more,
I do so pray,
Before the robin hops the snow
My hand in yours I find?

This year the holly bears many berries,
But what will Christmas be without dear Jonathan
Just in from the cold, a telegram waited my return,
No need to open to read the words -
Tomorrow we shall walk the woods together.

John Hopkins

FIRST LOVE

He felt the warmth of her kind eyes
He felt the love and care
He wanted to kiss her on the cheek
But knew he wouldn't dare.

Her hair was light and her eyes were blue,
Her mouth so rosy red.
He wanted her so very much
If only they could wed.

She touched his hand and smiled at him,
It filled his heart with glee
He looked at her and smiled right back,
Wondering if she could see

How marvellous he thought she was
How good and kind and true.
But, she was his teacher and he just a lad,
He wondered if she knew.

Oh, the days of fantasies and dreams
Yearning for the unknown.
Too soon those feelings will fade away,
Youth's passion having flown.

Linda Hurdwell

A New Spring Of Life

The Winter of my life is over,
a new Spring taking its place:
Love has sprung up like daffodils and tulips
that colour the countryside, with beauty and grace.

My new love's eyes sparkle like diamonds,
throwing their light into my heart:
The touch of her slender fingers upon my face
stir up passions, and my heart doth race.

As we are quietly strolling the country lanes
with arms entwining each other's waist,
I do not look at the stars in the sky -
her beautiful eyes, do take their place.

My life which of love has been so empty,
is now so filled with happiness and bliss
As my mouth seeks hers that is so pretty,
and when found, her lips, I do fervently kiss.

Geo K Phillips

Spanning The Years

We can fly, we can soar, there is no limit to how high,
over wooded misty valleys, across hilltops, under an azure sky.
Our love will remain forever, as the grey granite rocks of a tor,
together we can span the millennia, our love in our bodies
we'll keep and store.
Years spent with you seem like a split second, a mere dot
in the centuries,
is there nothing we cannot do, examinations of our love
will be just estimations, theories.
Through mirrored skies of sun, stars, and blue moons we sped,
our love for each other will never ever remain unsaid.

Brian Land

GIVE ME!

Give me the smiles on children's faces,
The sun and the sea in beautiful places.

Give me the sparkle in people's eyes,
The ecstasy in my lover's sighs.

Give me the laughter, from everyone's fun,
Lend me the moon, and give me the sun!

Give me the spring, and cycle of re-birth,
The tears in my eyes from all the mirth.

Give me the stars, and give me the trees,
The oceans, lakes, the rivers and the seas.

Give me the kiss of twenty five years, lost love,
The blessings and prayers from the heavens above.

Most of all, give me happiness and peace,
Until that time of my Spirit's release!

L M Pearson

WITHOUT LOVE

Never knowing love
Is missing something fine
Admiring the grapes
Yet never tasting wine
Loving then to lose
Brings such exquisite pain
Always there is hope
That love will come again
Better to have known
Just once to be enthralled
Even if love fades
Than not to love at all

Patricia Whittle

OVER YOU

Over you - I have cried
Over you - I nearly died
Over you - My heart was broken
Over words that by you were spoken
Over you - I've had time to think
Over you - I turned to drink
Over you - I lost my pride
Over you - My face did hide
Over you - I've tossed and turned
Over you - My love was spurned
Over you - I ache with pain
Over you - I won't love again
Over you - My heart was true
   I shall never get
    Over you.

Beryl Spanswick

LOVE OF MY LIFE

As we walk the path of life and deal with all it brings
We become involved with different people and
        experience many things
We learn how important it is to have a friend
Someone we can turn to, on whom we can depend
And if we're very lucky, as is the case with some
That friendship can turn into love, like this one has become
You're more than just my lover, my soul-mate and my friend
You're the one whom I'll share my life until it's at an end
I love you and I always will, there's nothing to compare
With this life we have together and the precious love we share

Andy Sullivan

MOONBEAMS

Through your bedroom windows tall
A light of softest hue will fall
On moonbeams high, and moonbeams low
Come dancing fairies on tiptoe.

Through moonbeams in, and out, they dance
Your slumbers to enhance
That little girl, oh moonbeams keep
So safe and warm, that she may sleep.

No shadows grace your face so fair
Your smile of love, be all you bear
In softness of your pillow keep
Your mind to rest, no tears to weep.

As moonlight beams toward the door,
On tiny feet they dance once more,
For she of beauty, there's only one,
Arrives the dawn and all have gone.

Of such enchantment I unfold
No fairy-tale, was ever told
It is no dream, my heart does keep
For I have seen those tiny feet
Along each moonbeam, whilst you sleep.

J M H Barton

YOU HEARD

you saw my tears, you heard my prayer
you gave your love for me to share
and the emptiness that was passed down to me
you filled with you, and set me free

Tyron Allbright

O GLORIOUS SPRING

When autumn gold turns to wintry brown,
And all the leaves come fluttering down,
When there's little warmth in the sun on high,
All life to ebb and some to die,
That mantle of white doth lay all around,
Stilling all growth and hushing all sound,
Mother Nature in her rest doth lay,
Waiting for the return of a springtime day,
Whence once again all life will stir,
The song of birds filling the morning air,
O glorious spring, cradle of life,
Whence all nature stems, even unto strife,
From thy womb all life is reborn,
Blessed by our Lord from thy earliest dawn,
O glorious spring.

W Barlow

WAIT AND SEE

We all need love, but who can say,
What we need at the end of the day.

Perhaps a cuddle or a warm embrace,
Even a little peck on the side of your face.

A squeeze of the hand, a whimsical smile,
Perhaps a helping hand on a sponsored mile.

But if you feel you have more than you need
Share it around and do a good deed.

We all need love you wait and see,
Your turn will come eventually.

Amelia Simms

LOVE POEM TURNS TRAGIC

That kiss upon my cheek,
Brings fullness as I speak,
I hear no loving words,
Just above the singing birds,
She has such heavenly powers,
I kissed her and gave her flowers.

In a soft voice, so low she replies,
Will you marry me? Was a real surprise.
Such youth and the happiest girl,
Reminds me of my mother's pearls.
So slim and light as the summer air,
I do love that long flowing hair.

Pleasure surges when she's around,
Her sweet life that nature found.
I glorified her in that mini dress,
My world right now full of gladness,
Hoping our real love won't change,
Things do change it's so strange.

This verse is the saddest part,
Hankies out it's going to break our hearts.
Into the path of a car, she tripped with her feet,
Sometimes fate takes a hand, something we all may meet.
Into the arms of God, is it really fate,
Sometimes we think loved ones are handed on a plate.

Philip Anthony Corrigan

TRUE LOVE

Our eyes met and I knew at a glance
We would fall in love at this meeting of chance,
Bringing happiness to my life and also to her
So I started to act and set things astir.

I wrote a letter asking her out on a date
Hoping that my effort was not too late
To persuade her that I was worthwhile to meet
And that I thought she was truly sweet.

She agreed that we meet to go out for a meal
To see how the land lay and how we did feel
About starting a courtship that could only be
The end of loneliness for her and for me.

Our love blossomed in no time at all
With the vicar having our banns to call.
We were up there floating on clouds of bliss,
Ending with that wonderful wedding kiss.

This all took place many moons ago
When we gave our love a chance to grow
By understanding each other's way of life,
And so we remain as man and wife.

Gerard Oxley

TOGETHER

Life can never be lonely, when you are with the one you love,
You enjoy all things together, like the moon and stars above.
When you do everything together, you are never on your own,
You enjoy each other's company in your loving home.

When your family have grown, and they have flown the nest,
You are then left together, and maybe enjoy some rest.
If you were left on your own, life could be sad,
But with your partner by your side, life is not so bad.

So you carry on with your life, side by side,
You've had many years together, since becoming groom and bride,
You enjoy your time together, the rest of your life,
There is nothing nicer in this world than being a loving
                                        husband and wife.

Stephanie Harvey

ALL THINGS BEING EQUAL

A cold soul-cleansing wind,
A carpeting of crisp snow
Shining like faceted quartz;
We come quietly upon the circle,
Caressing the craggy stones,
Participating in the grace.

I salute the sun some way off setting,
Then turn to see the cairn.
Violet clouds rush away
Exposing the almost full moon
Equal and opposite the sun.

Silently acknowledging
This sign of sacred magic,
I tell the child to make a wish
Moon to her left shoulder,
Sun to her right.

Issuing a blessing for all souls,
I smile, glad that we came.
Walking back along the snowy track,
The moon and sun stay equal
And opposite on either side,
Our companions to the stile.

A J Dixon

FIRESIDE GLOW

Lying beside your flame-kissed restful form
I feel your breasts against the stillness of my chest
And my hand plays softly along your thighs.
Night-time shadows speak to me of the taste of your lips
The fineness of your hair
The lure of your perfume
Whilst I blaze with desire for you.

Honeyed firelight surrounds your stretched composure.
Not glancing at me now,
Locked in your own rapt smile.
Heated by the moment
I hold you close and cling to passion's thrill.

The room slips further away like falling ash
Darkness confuses my gaze
But the tender warmth of you remains.

That rising stir of our bodies
Fades with evening memory.
Yet, stroking my cheek,
You reflect the loving glow in my eyes.

Chris Korta

CALVARY LOVE

Make more room in my heart for your love, Lord,
Let the striving of self fall away.
Work the miracle real deep within Lord,
Grant more love, yet more love, every day.

Hear my answer, my son: 'In your striving
Let the Spirit purge through your own soul.
There is much to refine to My likeness,
Learn of Me, if you'd be fully whole.

Then they'll recognise Me in your living,
My commandment to love will be kept.
Those I love will be reached by your giving;
Calvary love was revealed as I wept.'

I respond in a new-found surrender;
Give myself in a measure unknown.
Take my heart to infill with your love, Lord,
Then Your love through my living be shown.

Geoffrey Perry

DID I TELL YOU

Did I tell you that I love you
Did I say how much I care
Have I said that I am so lonely
And feel so lost when you're not there
Did I say how much I need you
In each and every way
To see you smile and hold your hand
I need that every day
Did I ever thank you
For all the years we've shared
Your patience and understanding
Showing that you cared
If I haven't told you
How much you mean to me
Now is the time to confess
Without you; where would I be?
You are my love
You are my life
I ask no more than to be
   Your wife

Rosemary Crowshaw

MY LOVE

Why is my love taken so lightly,
When my heart gives it so brightly,
My life with you, always feels right,
Don't ever leave me out of your sight.

My love for you is boundless,
My feelings know no end,
Your words are always soundless,
Must I be just a friend.

When our eyes meet, there is such a glow,
There are no words to say 'We know'
We always need to be together,
Let no one else make us dither.

If only you would hear my heart,
Telling you, we must not part,
No matter what others say,
We need each other, day by day.

I've grown to know you, need you, love you,
Want you with me all my life,
I feel that we were meant to be,
With each other to eternity.

If only you could put in words,
What I truly want to hear,
Tell me what you feel and long for,
Or is it really just a bore?

You have feelings, longings, true emotion,
Perhaps as deep as any ocean,
Tell me, tell me, what you need,
Do not think, I'll pay no heed.

I want to help you, guide you,
Always be there beside you,
To show you how life should be,
Always happy, come you'll see!

John L Pierrepont

ONE STEP NEARER TO GOD

I look into your eyes,
and the memories of a thousand lives
come flooding back to me from your gaze.
I know you as I know my own hand,
each crease representing
a time that we have spent together
in the perpetual school room of life.
I shall not be with you for much longer,
as my life on this plane is coming to an end,
but I no longer feel any remorse for leaving you,
for I have left you many times before
and I know that my destiny
will one day return me to your side.
Please do not mourn my death,
rather revel in my passing to a higher plateau,
a place where I will be one step nearer to God,
that omnipotent presence at the heart of reality
that binds us to the ether of our existence.
I will wait for you in that place,
just around the corner
in the ever-changing mists of time,
and look forward to the next life
when we will once more be together,
sharing the experience
of our journey to oblivion.

Susan Gifford

DON'T EVER LET IT GO

Love you cannot see it
Cannot hold it in your hand
And only when you feel it
Will you truly understand.

Love you cannot touch it
Or see it with your eyes
And when you really love someone
That true love never dies.

Love you cannot hear it
It's a whisper on the breeze
You only know that it is there
By the trembling of the leaves.

Love you cannot smell it
Only feel it in your soul
When someone gives love to you
Don't ever let it go.

K Brown

WILL TOMORROW BE SUNNY?

Magic is in the air
My darling is coming
Around the corner
In brilliant sunshine
Bringing hope for a pleasant future
When the rays of the sun disappear
Will my darling still be here
To keep the
Glow alive
Until we can rest
Together.

Pauline Finkleman

SONS AND DAUGHTERS LOST

As windows across the world are lit; this
thirteenth day of March, I wonder why it
has to be, that we have to light the lights
in memory of the little darling gifts of
joy, sons and daughters of the tree of
life sacrificed upon the altar of a sick
and lowly world by men with evil lurking in
their hearts, but like the seeds of the tree
of life their youth and beauty give us
dreams to dream, and although their flesh
has gone to dust; they will forever be with
us in the secret caverns of our hearts;
wayfarers of our tomorrows; walking roads
our human bonds forbid, upon the wind and
mountain top; the waves of boundless seas,
the spread of endless plains, soft whisperings
on sultry summer days. The fragrant smell of
earth when it has rained; all these things they
are to us and more, the twinkling stars up
there in space the immeasurable time of
timelessness, today's morning, tomorrow's dream;
the lovely smile on sunshine's face, little
darling gifts of joy ours only for a moment's
breath of life; our pleasure past our future
pain; the beginning of all things but not the
end; for our memories will carry them through
all the seasons that come and go. Sons and
daughters of the tree of life; gone from
us in flesh but never lost, for they will
forever occupy the souls and hearts of us,
shining like beacons on a sea of love as evil
does what evil does.

Martinella Brooks

DREAMERS

Dreamers' verses tailor-made,
Conscript written pages fade.
Horses flecked with grey-white dapples
Grass grows luscious, moist and precious.

Candle wavers in the draft,
Darkness shaky, cold and wan.
Moonlit streaks across our faces
Love walks out of empty spaces.

Slowly touching I move to you,
Kissing gently as soft as dew.
Wind sweeps through our tousled hair,
The sea brings in a blanket there.

Quilted forest moss awaits,
Tilted heads lay back to wake.
Silver rain refreshes faces,
Sunlit beams rejoin the spaces.

Warmness stirs our bodies,
Clay earth in our throats
Your moonlit face again I see
And your dwelling spirit moves in me.

Amanda Robbins

MEMORIES OF LOVE

Ever looked at a photograph
Of someone who's left you alone
You keep the memory alive
Your love for them has grown

Memories keep flooding back
You think of love and happiness
The tears you cry are all you have
There's no love; just sadness

The darker the night, the colder
A winter you'll never forget
There's no-one here to warm you
This time of year you both met

You fought to stay together
When love was on your side
No-one could have tried harder
To keep your love alive

Kevin McSkelly

A RAINBOW IN THE DISTANCE

All you need is love
To make the wheels of life go around,
It's simple and sweet when it's forward and kind,
But when something happens to trip one and leave
The sour taste of a love that has fled on the breeze
One needs the kind help of a dear, loving soul
To help you pick up, come in from the cold.

It can come in the form of a letter or call
To let you know you're not alone in the fall
It's encouraging how warmth, kind thoughts of a friend,
Can help ease the pain, you start over again.

So don't be discouraged if you've been let down
You feel life is awful and can't bear the sound
Of the mention of love, just what does it mean?
Start thinking of others, and you'll live life again.

For out in this world there is always someone
Who is worse off than you under the sun,
And with kind deeds and helping
You'll soon see again
The laughter of love and bright rainbows, less pain.

Elizabeth M Sudder

STATISTIC

I am bruised.
Like an orange
I have been squeezed dry.
I cannot cry
All the tears
Have been shed
and the bread
Cast upon the waters
Did not ease the famine.
Let us examine
The statistics
And try
to deny
that love
is in
short supply
this year!

Vicky Blake

YOUR FRIENDSHIP

Your friendship I have valued
and your kindness too,
the tears of laughter many,
the tears of heartache, few.
Yet, I've never known it hurt me
to say goodbye each day,
hear your door shut swiftly,
nor watch you walk away;
quite like today.

Susan Turner

TO ANN

Life hasn't been very good,
For you or me and I wish I could,
Make things better than they've been,
And give you a life you haven't seen,
The only thing I've been able to give,
From this useless body in which I live,
Is my love and I love you so much,
I long to hold you and feel your touch,
I love your kisses, your breath on my cheek,
Every day of every week,
I'm sorry I cause you so much pain,
I promise I'll try not to do it again,
I feel so useless in this body of mine,
Because that's what I am most of the time,
If there is a Lord up above,
All I ask of him is: 'Give me Ann's love.'

Alistair Howie

(11)

Men dream of women,
And women dream of men,
But dreams are only dreams.
Just as a mirage of an oasis in the desert
Does not feed the body of an Arab lost
                              in the sand dunes,
So do dreams not feed the longings of our appetites.
Dreams are only hopes,
And hopes have to be realised.
Only then we can burp with satisfaction
And say the banquet is a delight.

K R Sidhwa

MIND'S EYE

Through the window of your mind's eye
one inside that never cries
sees only this or that all the way to your heart
will do for a start.

Images unfold,
hidden beauty to behold
for the young and the old,
the meek as well as the bold.

Love can be seen
not in a dream
right before your very eyes,
all around starts.

Never ends,
you don't have to see
for real,
to feel.

Peter Richards

TO BELONG

My friends and I would climb a tree
Then their dad would shout 'Come for tea'
I'd go on home and give a wave
With a smile just to be brave.
My dad had left some years before,
And to my mum I seemed a chore,
But joy at last I've found a dad,
My children's dad I share,
He calls them in for tea
And one child who's left standing there.

P Sconce

Undiminished Love

Your hair once gold and silky
Now fine with threads of grey,
A face without a blemish once,
To me you'll always be that way.

Our courting days were long ago,
Yet still so fresh to me,
A love so loyal and true
Is ours eternally.

To me you are as beautiful
As on the day we met,
Each moment I have loved you more,
Not one do I regret.

You've been my lover and my nurse,
Born our children and loved them too,
My soul mate and best friend,
I love you through and through.

Now here with friends and family,
Eyes misted with our tears,
My heart is full of you alone
While we celebrate those fifty years.

Through many hardships we have been
Sorrow and ill-health too,
We've laughed and loved together,
Only, because you're you!

Though age has slowed us down a lot,
Our love has altered, not a jot,
We've lots more good times yet to come,
Life is good, we two are one.

M Gardner

Sweet Memories

If we never meet again, I don't know what I'd do
I just cannot go on through life without ever seeing you
My heart it aches so much my love, this feeling never goes
I miss your laugh, I miss your smile, my beautiful English rose

Your hair so soft with scent anew, your eyes so deep and true
sweet memories within my heart are always there of you
Why should I worry, why should I care, why do I miss you so
why does it rain, why does it shine, why does it even snow?

These questions I have asked myself so many times I'm sure
this pain, this hurt, this heartache, so much do I endure
Go on with life they say to me, forget her, leave her be
but they don't know what's in my heart or what you mean to me

Your photo stands here next to me, beside me as I sleep
the one that you alone gave to me, the one I'll always keep
I cannot turn it around, nor can I put it away
as I want to always remember you this day and every day

For one day darling maybe, my dreams will all come true
and you will then come back to me and we can start anew
I keep this dream locked in my heart, no-one will ever know
that darling I just love you, like green the grass does grow.

B S Berger

An Old Love Song

The song has ended
It was a favourite old refrain,
And I know I won't hear her sing it again.

The voice that cheered and thrilled my day
As it sang so sweet and tenderly,
Can only now be heard in halting whispers.

Yet, the haunting memory that's left behind
Still echoes down the lane of time,
And through the storms and strains of life
Brings back again our days of bliss.

The song that ended
Was a favourite old refrain.
Oh, that I could hear her sing it again.

Alex Goodwin

ALL ALONE AT TWILIGHT

I look out of my window
When night begins to fall.
All alone at twilight
Waiting for love's call.

The crescent moon up in the sky
Shines down upon my face.
It makes my teardrops glisten
From its home way out in space.

The first star begins to twinkle
Beneath that bright new moon.
And shadows they start falling
On the four walls of my room.

The silence it surrounds me
Except the whisper of the breeze
Silhouettes far away in the distance
Of chimney pots and trees.

But then the sound of childish laughter
An aeroplane in the sky.
Yet I'm still alone at twilight
And all alone I cry.

Joanne Frampton

THE TREE OF LOVE

I sit here by my telephone
And wait for it to ring.
I'm happy but I'm also sad.
What news will it bring?

My heart is beating like a drum
It's louder than a clock.
I sit here waiting patiently
And then I hear a knock.

What do I do, what can I say?
Will he turn and go?
Or will he stay with me,
So that our love can grow?

If he stays our love will blossom,
And I'll know that he'll be mine
But if he goes, my love will die.
And I've lost him for all time.

So if you look at all the trees,
And there's no fruit to see.
You'll know how many loves have lost.
To be lonely just like me.

L Allen

SOLILOQUY FOR A LOST LOVE

Why did you have to go
When with my heart I loved you so,
When with my eyes I loved to see
Your love reflected back to me.

When with my ears I loved to hear
The magic of your voice so dear.
Could I but hear that voice again
'Twould banish sorrow - ease the pain!

Why did you have to go,
When with my soul I loved you so,
And why had all those blissful years
To end, for me, in bitter tears!

Celia White

BLUE TANGO

'Shall we dance?'
With firm young hand you clasped my own
a fleeting life-time since.

I hold it now
that same loved hand
cool, ashen, highly veined
and stroking, ease its gentle shake.

In passion I caressed your face
those ardent years ago
firm cheekbones
in so confident a sculpture.

Touching now
familiar and dear
I trace your tissue skin
and softly map its tell-tale lines
as sadness overwhelms me

but soon you wake
and gaze into my old eyes
then from a never ageing love
I hear 'Blue Tango'
and we, not stirring
dance our dance again.

Rita E A Stephenson

BIRTHDAY LOVE LETTER

Dear Zoë,

You visited me today, but not *one* word
did I hear you say.
You listened and looked with those bright blue eyes.
Your call came early and took me by surprise.
You entered this world only *one* week ago
Zoë sweet baby, I do love you so.
Let me explain just how you came,
Before your person became a name.
'Twas Friday noon the second of May
When you decided to make headway
You wriggled and wrestled (to warn your Mum)
For on brother J's birthday you decided to come.
Yes, true to time your arrival took place,
I looked down with love to your tiny face.
Perfection, completed, proudly adored,
Zoë - a birthday gift - with love from our Lord!

Love Grandma Pam

P Holland

DISTANCE

Within a past existence
       Beside a tideless sea
My love said, 'Infinite distance
       For future hope have we.'

In space and time's resistance
       Across another sea
I cried, 'My love, the distance
       Is your long doubt of me!'

Jessie Lamont

IT COULD BE YOU

I died in my sleep
And woke up in Hell
I watched my last penny
Sink in the well

Make a wish
And hope it comes true
Don't let the dream die
It could be you

I sold my soul
For a slice of fun
And played Russian roulette
With a full chamber in the gun

I didn't know who to turn to
Or who I could trust
I believed I was made of steel
But I just crumbled to rust

I gave up on humanity
And walked an endless mile
I never thought I would feel happy again
Until I saw your smile

Is it too late?
For a sinner to repent
You look like an angel
You must be Heaven sent

You restored my faith
And brought me back to life
You're the one that pulled me through
And maybe one day I'll tell you.

Sean Brown

WITHIN THIS DREAM

Floating on a sea of tranquil stillness
  In the abundance of no pain
    Within this mind and distant shores
      Of these feelings the mind is where

Lost to the joys of all believing
  Drifting through such lasting thoughts
    Of such things or being what
      On the roads in dreams and seems

Laying and hearing such watery sounds
  Constant slapping within thy mind
    Endless joys in peaceful stillness
      Being all to one who dreams

Take me towards thy open door
  Within such dreams thou are mine
    Of this joy lost unto love
      Are these arms around and around

What is said within this mind
  Unreal and should come unto me
    Of these feelings and loving passion
      In the mysteries of living dreams

Let thy Venus come and anoint
  In the realms of thousand lives
    Drifting through such earthly births
      As being one with whom and who

All so lost within this dream

E T Ward

WISHES

(To my husband Bill)

I wish I was eighteen again
When I danced to the sound of Glen Miller's band
And joy and heartbreak went hand in hand
And love was an old refrain.

I wish I was twenty-one again
When my heart was won and love was strong
And days were short and nights were long
And blessed babies came.

I wish I was thirty-five again
When there was laughter more than tears
Wolf whistles fell upon my ears
And life was just a game.

I wish I was forty-two again
With children grown but the nest not flown
And teenage love needed a shoulder to cry on
And I was once again sixteen.

I wish I was fifty-three again
When love once more taught my heart to sing
And I let it fly on gossamer wing
To your heart's safe haven.

At sixty-six, my total sum,
Of wishes now I have no need
With you, my love, to gently lead -
The best is yet to come.

Heida

MARRIAGE WITH A PARALYTIC

Such love was theirs,
Love rarely found in woman or in man.
Though he could never clasp her in his arms,
His words were as sweet music in her ears
And, from his eyes, there shone a burning light
That warmed her heart and met her inmost need,

Her tender look,
Compassionate and yet admiring too,
Rejoiced his soul - she was so proud of him.
She was his life, all that he could not be,
Thinking and feeling as he thought and felt,
Bound to him in a mystic union.

Both one in Christ,
They shall not fear what time the fragile clay
Crumbles to dust, for loving still remains -
To be enriched, one day, beyond their dreams,
When human love at last shall reach perfection
And that which is *in part* be done away.

May Griffith Edwards

I DON'T MIND

I don't mind if there is nothing, there's always you,
I don't mind if there is pain, there's always you,
I don't want to give it to anyone else, only you,
my dreams my aspirations, just you.

Wake up in the morning, with you,
watch a film without yawning, thanks to you.
In all my bitter pains of life, I thank God there's you.
You have been my inspiration, my guest,
my long woolly stockings, and the rest.

Thanks for the heartbeat, support, and friend,
you have made my life worth living right to the end.
You ask for no money, no crystal gaze kiss,
just my love to be funny, with days made of bliss.

M K Lynch

I LOVE TO SEE

I love to see flowers in bloom;
To note their form; the sweet perfume;

The buzzing bees; grass's green shades;
The rising sun; sky, when day fades;

A fresh ploughed field; the waving corn;
The freshness of a dewy morn;

Pale mellow moon; a twinkling star;
Fast-scudding clouds; mountains afar;

The shapes of trees; a bird that sings;
Rushing water; butterflies' wings;

The restless waves; ships in full sail;
Long summer days; a creeping snail;

The countryside; a quiet lane;
Reflecting glass, and porcelain;

Happy children; and laughing eyes;
True affection; a nice surprise;

The things you say; the things you do;
The way you are; you being you;

But most of all, I love to see,
The smile upon your face for me.

H Val Horsfall

A SIMPLE CURE

What do you need when you feel low
when you're late for work and your car won't go
What do you need when the sun won't shine
and last night's guests have drunk the wine
What do you need when the plants won't grow
the grass is long and needs a mow
What do you need when the post in the door
hasn't the letter you're waiting for
What do you need when the children cry
and you can't find the reason why
What do you need for all these things
to make a play on your heart strings
What you need is lots of love
All you really need is love.

Isobel Clanfield

WISHING ON A STAR

Wishing on a star,
dreaming out a dream,
feeling this true love,
what does this all mean?
Hearts are filled with warmth,
arms are safe, secure,
whatever this love is
I just want more and more,
slipping into sleep,
your face is in my mind,
this is my true love,
for no-one else to find.

Allison Hughes

A LOVE IN POEM

Love is love
Love is here to stay,
Love me all the time boy
He will show the way;
We have a good anchor
In anyone's mind,
Travelling north south east and west
Nothing left behind;
Anything could have happened
So don't worry about a thing,
We will always be happy
With all the joys of living;
Never mind about the hassle
Don't listen to flapping tongues,
Love belongs to love
Like the very breath in your lungs;
Each day that passes by
Will never be our last;
For after this life ends
The next one will be, the new task.

Amy Hogan

TRUE COMMUNION

To see you smile when by chance we meet
This heart of mine would truly make replete
For even though we are together only moments fleet
True souls should ever each other with gladness greet
With no diminishment, reproof or a dismissal neat
For doth not charity and goodness fill all of judgement's seat
And therefore makes us both and all complete?

David Viall

UNTITLED

Winter came
With cruel, painful death.
Faces pale
We walked along the gritty track
Dad and me.
Past blood-red yew berries
Bitter holly leaves.
Dad, feeling the way with his stick,
            over the rough ground.
Straight for his age.
Smart checked jacket.
Medical corps tie.

Almondbury cemetery,
Rows of headstones
Waiting patiently for visitors.
Frost dusted moors all round.
How pretty the grave looked.
A riot of joyful colour -
Like a little cottage garden!
It took me by surprise.

We added our roses
Then stood in silence
One on each side
Grief swallowing us.

Elaine Dunwell

A WORLD WITHOUT LOVE

Just imagine having a world without love.
No romance. No roses. No cards.
No joyful moments or memories to store
in one's heart, for when times get hard.

No tender nursing when a hospital bed
is cold and you're left all alone.
No comforting hand, or encouraging word.
Just unfeeling hearts made of stone.

No one there in the house to welcome you in
after a long day out at work.
No cheerful voice asking, 'Cup of tea love?'
So tidy. Not one spider lurks.

I feel for those people who've never known love,
Glowing warmth of comforting arms.
Its passions, its feelings, hurts too it can bring.
Above all is love's peace. Like balm.

Joyce Monks

LOVE

Love is a smile
Love is a look
Love is a passion
Love is calm
Love is a storm
Love is laughter
Love is tears
Love is tender
Love is hard
Love is a word
Love is life.

Lynne Gavaghan

LOVE AWAKENING

We stand apart and yet our hearts
extend fingertips and our humours
intermingled cascade iridescently
through the labyrinths of our minds
bathing our innermost thoughts in
new awareness that shakes the very
seat of the soul

intoxicated in the effluvia of love
our nostrils dilate
to savour the wonder of it
our flesh is flushed with blood
and our lips thus engorged
tremble as they meet

all around us dims into insignificance
and we made bold by this encounter
meet more fiercely and yet still restrained
our hands are possessive of the other
and with their movements seek to convey
the feelings that are within ourselves

dear God these pent-up emotions must
explode within our bodies and joined
as we are flesh to flesh
it is doubled in its intensity and thus
devoid of energy we lie
in each other's arms
and can only wonder

Ben Warren

CHRISTMAS LOVE
(For Badger)

Sad eyes, filled with pain
Your heart, heavy with loss
Touches me deeply
It's Christmas

Feeling helpless and inadequate
I watch you hurting inside
Powerless to intervene
I'll hold you close

Though I'm here for you, always
A lover and a friend
It is pain I can't reach
Making me sad

A loner, needing someone, sometimes
To fill the void that's in you
Let it be me
This Christmas.

Kathy Jacques

MORNING SONG

Come, come my darling one,
Some tea, to rise and shine.
To leave a kiss, within the cup,
Would be the perfect sign,
That love to me, is pure and true,
Love to me, is strong,
Our partnership is ever more,
And everlasting long.

Sara Russell

COLOURS

Green is just the gentleness
Like grasses in the breeze.
Blue, straightness and honesty
And little things that please.
Thoughtfulness is lavender
And the deepest midnight blue.
Is the depth of my emotion
That I feel when I'm with you.
Yellow for the sunshine
That surrounds me when you're near.
Red, it signals danger
From which you keep me clear.
Oranges and browns do
The warmth of autumn bring.
White it makes our love so pure
Gives my heart a little ring.
Black is the darkness of the night
When you're away.
But then it turns to gold
At the start of a new day.
Purple for the shade
Of unhappiness I find.
When worries seem to linger so
And chase across my mind.
Turquoise is a pastel
Neither green nor blue.
It comes when there's decisions
To be made by me or you.
Silver is the brightness
That you bring into my life.
All these colours come together
When I become your wife.

J Vale

UNREQUITED LOVE

I would dearly, dearly like to know,
The secrets of your mind,
Was that an admiring glance in your eyes,
Or, just your good self being kind!

Did I misunderstand that certain look,
That passed between when we met,
Was it perhaps a blurred illusion,
A moment's sweet wonder, and yet?

I felt there was an affinity there,
Like a touch of a butterfly's wing,
A feeling rare that cannot describe,
The lift in the hearts upsurging.

Your thoughtful concern is real enough,
A greeting always sincere,
Just a brush of a kiss upon my cheek
Are moments of bliss I hold dear!

What joy it would be to feel you near,
Easing my mind where much doubt lies,
But knowing you are bound to another,
Seals my lips and blinds my eyes!

I vow to dismiss you from my mind,
So unwary thoughts will be stilled,
I'll neatly pack my dreams in a drawer,
Where they will remain unfulfilled!

Joan Clift

To The One I Love

You are the first dew-hung flower
That opens in the morning sun;
You are the gentle breeze
That parts the whispering rush;
You are the noonday sun that
Gives voice to the skylark;
You are the bright red sunset
That promises a bright new dawn;
You are the night sky alive
With glittering stars;
You are mine, and I love you.
Please hurry home!

Lucy Crisp

A Date

When going to meet the one we love
We all take special care
The time we spend to look just right
On clothes we wear and our hair

When at last we are ready to go
With excitement deep inside
The love we feel for the one we love
We sometimes try to hide.

At last we meet with joy in our hearts
And love shines in our eyes
Together we will be happy now
'All you need is love' you sigh.

Margaret Proctor

INFIDELITY

Please read this letter
Don't just throw it away
It took a long time to write
Almost a year to the day
The same length of time
Since I first saw you there
Under the clock
In the town centre square
About the same time
You came into my heart
Although we've never been together
We've never been apart.

So I'm begging you now
Will you meet up with me
We'll have a chat about it
And hopefully we'll see
If anything can come
From my feelings for you
Nothing dirty or sordid
But beautiful and new.

But you must let me know
If you're meeting me there
Under the clock
In the town centre square
If you don't I'll give up
On this whole crazy plan
I'll stay at home with my missus
And you with your old man.

Leslie W Booth

NIGHTMARE

My mind travels with ease
Packed with treasured memories
Back to whence I came
Home with Mum and Dad.

Rock rock with the heartbeat,
Mummy's girl under the sheet
Eyes play with patterns on the wall
Till sleep her net do trawl.

I wake, eyes peep, really it's a disgrace
Gone patterns pretty colours and shape
Skin prickles with cold sweat, of fear
Now unfriendly grey shadows bunch, point, and sneer.

Horror, I see a person I most dread
At the bottom of my bed, *Bogy Man*
Dressed in black, thin, pointed chin, tall hat
He reaches out to get me, I sob *Mum.*

Swift to come, black Tibs too.
Bold warrior mother mine
Long lance, steady flight
Routs the dreary dreads of night

Hushed, tucked, and sweetly kissed,
Fear is instantly dismissed
Love's murmurings low lead to slumbers deep.
All you need is love.

Joyce Barry

SOMEONE

Somewhere in a dream there's Someone
Making all my dreams come true
Somewhere in this world with Someone
Maybe it's someone like You!

Somewhere in my dream there's somewhere
Where the sky is always blue
Somewhere where I'll find my Someone
In a world just made for two.

Dreaming our dreams together
Our world will always be
Just for we two, forever
Somehow we'll always be -

Somewhere in our world in Somewhere
Where my dreams of you come true
Something in my heart keeps singing
Somewhere with Someone like You!

Nelson Peters

MUSE

You write me my life,
I just pick up the pen
And 'lo and behold' you are off again.
Sometimes it's funny, sometimes it's daft,
It's thoughtful and deep when the moment is right.
I'd be lonely without you and lost for ideas,
You gladden my heart and dry up my tears.
Who are you? They ask
And I smile from within,
Shall I tell them my love?
No - I'll pick up my pen.

Brenda Dove

THIS MAN

This man who lays beside me is mine,
Though we both know he never can be.
But he is mine, in a way,
For these few precious hours.
He looks content, head resting on the pillow,
Dark hair tousled from sleep,
Eyes still closed to the new day,
The new day of our lives.

I wonder, will he still feel the same?
Still care as much, now?

He seems to sense my gaze upon him.
Eyes still closed, his strong arm
Moves slowly across the sheet
Until it touches mine.
His warm, soft hand, the hand I've touched
So many times before
Tenderly closes over my hand,
And I feel secure.

He turns his head, eyes open now.
Our eyes lock in the gaze that says
Everything.
There is no need to speak, but we do,
Only to confirm what is being said.
Is he really saying the words that are
So important to me?
The words I doubted I would ever hear again.
'I love you,' he whispers, gently squeezing my hand.
'I love you,' I smile, unable to hide
The joy he has given me.
Yes, I am his until eternity, and he is mine,
This man who lays beside me,
For the first and last time.

Kay Spurr

SEASONS OF LOVE

The growing signs of early spring
The joy that new born life can bring
Birds that sing and lambs that play
The glory of a summer's day

Sweet-scented flowers that bees adorn
And sunlit fields of ripened corn
Speckled autumn leaves of gold
The beauty as the year grows old

The silence of a winter night
With moon so full and stars so bright
Dark silhouettes of leafless trees
You my love are all of these

David Guy Prosser

A LONG AGO LOVE

I loved you once and now you've gone
A searing love like summer's heat;
Then autumn came and dead leaves fell
To lie like stardust at my feet.
A shimmering dream of what once was
Like crescent moon with halo fine;
Like ripples widening on a pool
'We'll love,' we said, 'to the end of time.'
But when love fades and nothing's left
And we have gone our separate way;
Thoughts converge in glutinous mass
Submerging dreams into moist decay.

Joanne White

TEARS WITH EVERYTHING

Remember when we were lads and lassies,
And saw the world through rose-coloured glasses?
Up the church aisle, by friends we were spied.
Facing the future all dewy-eyed -
Then arrived our first babe - a boy;
So many tears of love and joy.
Anniversaries followed, how the years quickly pass,
We richly were blest with three lads and a lass,
It wasn't easy as they grew tall and strong,
Explaining the difference between right and wrong.
We shared disappointments and many fears,
Usually resolved with a cuddle and tears,
They're grown now, and fine folks they are,
Surpassing our prayers for each of them by far -
We've cried at their weddings, and graduations too.
Now history is repeating as future comes into view.
We have two lovely grandchildren, and two more soon to be
Please could someone reach for the tissues
        and pass them over to me.

Ilean Greig

SIMPLY LOVE

When life gets tedious, boring and dull
All we need to live life to the full is love
A handclasp, a kiss, a tender embrace
These are the things that help us to face
Life's traumas and cares we all know now and then
Love overcomes them again and again
That priceless ingredient sent from above
Makes us all realise all we need now is love.

Cathie Bridger

FEBRUARY 14TH

On the mat, in the
morning, four
envelopes,
one brown, two
white, one
red.
Childlike, leave
red
till last, finger
it with
unexpected glee -
ready now
glasses
on . . .

The address is mine,
the name
is not.
She must be disappointed, too.

Jan Wild

TOO OLD TO LOVE?

If I had a mouth
For every one of your grey hairs,
I'd spit in my eyes a thousand times
To wipe them clean of the pictures
Of my broody mares
That once cantered joyously
Around our young, green feather-filled field
Melding your browns with mine.

Janice Martin

Affairs Of The Heart!
Pain At Three AM

As I sit on my own at 3 am,
My heart's shattered,
The woman I loved has left me,
My world with a hammer, battered.

I feel this pain that I can't see,
This pain all twisted and deep,
At times love is the enemy,
This pain is why I don't sleep.

I've written some words in a letter,
I tried, tried to get her here,
Tried, so hard to make it better,
As my love for her was so sincere.

But as the reality is coming round,
I feel her voice in a sound,
As it echoes down the street,
What we had is no more . . .
But what we had was sweet.

C Gordon

Untitled

I imagine you hold me in the night
And clasp me against you tight,
Your tiny kisses against my hair
Remind me you are there.
Your warm hands on my bare skin
Wonder where to begin
And then it all seems to fade
Before our love could be made.

Elizabeth H Walter

ONE-SIDED LOVE

When my daily love is so one-sided
And not thus returned, as though not there
I now beweep my outcast state instead
Of rejoicing in life's beauty to share.
Love smiles gently at some in gentle youth
Now like spring nature gives youth true blossom
At this young age, they roam the world aloof
And the opposite gender are welcome,
As mortal age wears away life's beauty
Facial lines appear, forming wrinkled brow
Thus ageing, life seems not so easy
Life frowns, steeply showing her twisted trail.
Mind never ages, not understood as yet
Youth and elderly show little respect.

Leon Gould

APHRODITE

I watch her perfect form,
sculpted flesh and bone,
more beautiful than marble statue.

Ethereal image of ancient Greece,
Goddess of Love
standing on rocky outcrop.
Robe, purest white caresses her body,
a gentle whisper in the breeze.
Outlined temple on distant hill,
waves lapping about her feet,
watched by an evening sun
as she gazes out to sea.

She is my Aphrodite.

P M Fuller

YOU CALL MY NAME

How I cherish our first moments spent together
Kindness for a stranger on the production line
A young pure innocent smile thrills, is priceless
Your words will live forever, sweet vintage wine.

I have never felt such affinity with a girl
You listened in awe of my achievements in life
I felt desire, so flattered by strong attention
You inspired romantic dreams of a wonderful wife.

Each day my heart skipped a beat thinking of you
One glimpse flew me where I work hard to be,
One of the girls yet your eyes flickered across
To ignite a blazing fireball no one could see.

Our dinnertime walks to fish and chip shops
Gave more pleasure than my life's burdens tolled
Warm cheeks, sweet smile, gentle words, dark hair
Pieces of your heart steal all value from gold.

Every day, night I picture your face in my mind
Where once flew a spark now burns eternal flame
I walk like a man, keep faith until the time
My spirit flies to our place, you call my name.

John Farrell

SOUVENIRS

Looking through the souvenirs
Of a love that lies behind me,
I find I can't hold back the tears
A melancholy finds me.

The tickets to a West End play
Are crumpled and all torn,
The roses pressed between two books
So withered and forlorn.

The record that reminds me of
The time we danced all night,
The ribbons tied around the cards
And notes he used to write.

But now I will start to dry my eyes
And think about my new love,
And throw away the souvenirs
That remind me of an old love.

Patricia Frampton

AFTER THE FLOOD

I can't go on believing you'll stay
and I can't forget you, love's in the way
but I can still hope you'll think of me.
I loved you, if only you'd see.

Running in circles it's always the same
if we take chances, who'll take the blame?
The past seems so bad, a future not bright
it's so hard to get through the night.

Tossing and turning, my mind is a blur
pointing of fingers and threats we incur.
As sad as I am, I still miss your touch,
something so right, shouldn't hurt so much.

I need some sunshine, I need to smile
I want to be happy, if just for a while.
We live and go on, as tough as it seems
hoping someday to live all our dreams.

Someone to laugh with, share all your tears
someone - a soulmate, you've not known for years
with feelings so strong and emotions so high.
It's so very hard to let the past slip by.

Edita M Agee

LOVING EYES

My eyes glanced around the ballroom floor,
I stopped at the handsome man by the door,
Our eyes meet my temperature rose,
The whole of my body then just froze,
It was love, yes love at first sight,
I knew within he was Mr Right,
He walked towards me across the room,
I knew that shortly we would be bride and groom,
His eyes were sparkling he had a nice smile,
He spoke to me gentle, shall we dance for a while,
Words were not spoken I was in his arms,
We danced a spin waltz I was in a trance,
I will never forget the moment we met,
In my life I have no regret,
That day our eyes met across the room,
It was like red rose in full bloom.

Teresa Walker

I CAN RECALL

I can recall when first we met
Above a pub called the Bird's Nest.
I can recall when we first danced
My heart had not known such romance.
I can recall when we first held hands
And walked together on Seaton sands.
I can recall when our lips first touched
I can recall how much I blushed.
I can recall all that has passed
'Cos how I felt will always last.
So thanks Nigel for all that's gone
And I look forward to what's to come.

Sharon Goodall

LOVE IS -

He sang and played guitar
Entertaining the evening crowd
Sitting and eating on the promenade,
And he saw her strolling along,
Love is -

So late every night he came to play
Beneath her balcony window,
Romantic ballads, love songs
And Romany gypsy serenades,
Love is -

She lingered and looked,
She listened and laughed,
She ignored him all through,
He became depressed,
Love is -

This went on all summer
Even when it rained,
And the raindrops fell as still he played
With the rain dripping from his hair,
Love is -

The raindrops fell like falling tears
And melted her heart,
And that was the night he ran away
With Elizabeth Jane,
Love is -

Esme Francis

LOST IN YOU

My love I am lost in you,
and now I fear I can never untwine
our hearts, for in this breast this beating
I am unsure if it's yours or mine.

Inside my soul are thoughts of only you
and moments without you I can do naught but pine
for I hear your voice within me soft and low
and long till once more my eyes are locked in thine.

'Tis true tho' all the beauteous sights I've seen
none are as wondrous as your face when it looks in mine
some say there are seven wonders of the world
shouldn't purest love and trust make it nine?

And still now our love grows on
like two young berries growing on a leafy vine
our love has ripened
and become a sweet mature wine.

Susan Stewart

YOUR SMILE

A smile so warm and friendly,
Makes grey skies drift away,
Such sweet and tender beauty,
Your smile makes any day.

Your smile makes the sunshine,
Picks me up if I feel blue,
To see a smile so radiant,
The smile that comes from you.

Dave Maxfield

MY DREAM

I wonder shall we meet again, in my dreams tonight
We very often do my dear when all is dark and quiet
I've met you in some places where I have never been
And other times and places that before I've never seen
In my dream I met you beside a waterfall
Misty spray hung in the air, a mocking bird did call
Sunlight changed the silver spray to a glittering cascade
Of scintillating jewels, rubies, pearls and jade
We strolled along hand in hand, toward a rocky ledge
It disappeared from our view as we approached the edge
We kissed, you turned, stepped through the waterfall
The only thing I could hear was the echo of my call
The dream was over, you were gone, but not before we had planned
To meet again another night, in wonderful dreamland
So when my dream returns my dear, it will be of you
And maybe, who can tell, my dream might just come true.

Charles Serbert

LOVE

What would we do without love
The love you have for your mum and dad
The love you have for a child or a pet
Without love what would we do

When you fall in love
The world becomes a different place
You walk around with a smile on your face
Your heart feels light and bright

How long love will last no-one knows
Sometimes it just grows and grows
When you fall in love it all depends
But when you do you'll hope it never ends.

J Pearson

EVERYWHERE IN MY LIFE

You are still everywhere in my life
No matter where I go or what I do
I am always thinking of you
Each day and long night through
A piece of my heart is now missing
And I long to complete it again
It has left me so alone and so empty
Silent tears, heartache, and pain
But, memories of you keep returning
Of lovely times spent in the past
I can keep these memories forever
Or, for as long as my life will last
For when we meet again in God's time
There will be no more struggles or strife
When once again you will be everywhere
Everywhere each day in my life.

Marie Hodges

BY CHANCE

Met him, only by chance,
In fact, just a 'fleeting' glance!
It was love at first sight,
I *knew* it was right.
Wouldn't last, friends did say,
We had a wonderful Wedding Day!
It did last, our love is stronger,
Since we met, all those years ago,
Soon our Golden Wedding, you know!
It *was* love at first sight.
And I proved them right,
By chance!

Pauline Harper

IN MY THOUGHTS

When I wake up;
When I shower;
When I dress;
When I eat breakfast;
When I drive to work;
When I *try* to work;
When I have lunch;
When I drive home again;
When I have dinner;
When I watch TV,
(or read a book);
When I go to bed;
When I go to sleep

I dream of you . . .

Always.

Frances McHugh

A STOLEN KISS

I stole a kiss a simple kiss
last night, my wife was sleeping
a simple kiss that meant so much
and truly worth life keeping.

I stole a kiss a simple kiss
just as my wife was waking
a simple kiss of meaning
that truly was worth taking.

James Hope (Deceased)

DREAMS OF VANESSA

Love is like
Living in a golden universe
Love is like
Holding sunlight in your arms
You feel all warm inside
You feel without it you will die
Oh to be in love

Rainbows shine
All about your soul
Rainbows shine
From behind melting brown eyes
Your heart flutters light
You can't sleep still at night
Oh to be in love

Kisses sweet
Like honey upon the breeze
Kisses sweet
As silk pressed upon my skin
Your heart feels aglow
You want the world to know
Oh to be in love

Emotions are
The waves upon the shore
Emotions are
The whims and vexes of your moods
With your touch they are to please
With your hold I am at ease
Oh to be in love

Love is knowing
To taste the scent of a rose
Love is knowing
A touch so soft it hurts
You breathe laughter into my heart
I could never let us part
Oh to be in love

Anthony Day

TO YOU

You lie there sleeping next to me
I ask myself, 'How could this be?'
My heart and I reply with glee,
'Because you had a taste for me.'

And when you told your love to me
'What' I asked, 'would our children be?'
You answered me determinedly,
'Why half of you, and half of me.'

You've been to me the truest friend
I know you will be to the end
You do not take, you only give
Yes you have taught me how to live.

So tell to me my friend, my love
Although you call me 'turtledove',
Is it what you hoped it'd be?
Bare your soul and let me see.

J J Peacock

THE MAGIC OF LOVE

Love touches your soul,
It clutches your heart,
Positive feelings right
From the start.

Waves of emotions entwined
Deep within,
Equally shared, with a half
Cheeky grin.

A warm glow surrounds you,
From near and afar,
Like gliding through space
As a wandering star.

Love finds a way, when true
And sincere, with tender
Moments, you can hold dear.

This wondrous joy is there
To be found.
Just stop a minute, and do
Look around.

Love has no measure - no
Scales - and no time,
magical mountains, we all
Need to climb.

Of friendship and laughter,
That is so crystal clear.
And who knows what *you* will
Be doing *next year.*

Janice Gilbert

LETTER TO JOHN

Thanks for a sweet letter and lovely photo
Your kind of bloke is hard to find at all,
It will be great getting to know you well
I'll be your Cinderella, take me to the ball!

Forget all other men, I'll try for you!
Nice eyes, dark hair, my type of man,
Romantic, kind, genuine - that's better still
We must meet soon, make sure we can!

I wish we were adults in the sixties
You'd love my blouse, boots and mini-skirt
Listen to the Beatles, Stones, have fun
Would you wear a suit and frilly shirt?

A winter weekend in the 'Lakes' sounds great
Can I hear your record collection one day?
Do you honestly like brown-haired girls, John?
Write soon, we've got so many things to say.

Bernadette Lawless

LOVE YOU . . . !

Kiss my fingers
Kiss my nose,
How I tingle to my toes.
Stroke my hair
Be aware I'm there -
Listen to my woes.

Your turn to stay in bed,
Eggy breakfast, soldier toast?
Beloved, tell me true
Who's indulged the most . . ?

Joanne Manning

TO PETRA, OUR DAUGHTER
(On her 21st birthday)

One and twenty years to Heaven,
out of the cradle,
onto the sea
of life, grown up:
God guide your craft;
though sick betimes,
your courage last.

Sail, not drift,
to the other side of life mature:
Enjoy the ride;
but know yourself,
you have the key
to make or mar your destiny.

John Maisey

LOVE

Love is the twinkle in your eye,
Love is the ache in your heart.
Love is togetherness.

Love is when you fall,
And having someone to pick you up,
Love is a ball.

Love hurts when you quarrel and shout,
Love hurts when there is no one else about.
Love hurts when you walk through the door,
Love hurts when there is no love left anymore.

Margaret Coleman

LOVE

When love is filled with happiness,
And two hearts are filled with gladness,
When love is full of bliss, that only lovers know,
When two in love share their first kiss, then that affection will grow

Such love, and wonder, and the ecstasy
Is such a fragile thing, like two white doves that fly so free,
Or like swallows flying with their strong wings,
Or like a shadow of a little sparrow, that sweetly sings.

Like churchbells that chime so merrily.
The sweet melodious sounding so heartedly,
To bring the good news all around,
To know that God is everywhere, and His greatest love is found,

To the radiant love that grows, that only God can put together
Through the innocence of romance, and the attachment that lasts for
ever,
Never to be abused or neglected,
Never to be misguided or regretted,

Such love, when two couples are lost in the magic of a kiss,
It's far beyond knowing, how hearts can know such joy and bliss,
For, if two in love are sure and true,
There will be the blessedness, and good fortune, too,

True love will never part, for good or worse, they say,
God alone can teach us, the real meaning of love, through His way,
Then two hearts are filled with gladness, and love will surely grow,
Like the life of a stream, that will currently drift, and forever flow,

Like the two white doves that gracefully fly,
Like the truest love that is fragile, but, surely will never die,

J P McGovern

If Only

loved without loving
seen without seeing
a wish
for me
alone
flushed
hot
red
unseen yet
looking

a desire
for you
unmet
sighed
long deep
unheard yet
listening
loved without loving
seen without seeing

Anne Saunders

First Love

If I should write a poem of love
then it would be of the first,
for that one we remember
and nothing takes its place.

There is no hand as gentle
as that clasped in our own,
and strolling through the twilight
no cares or fears are ours.

The words that pass our lips
are tender and always true,
for young hearts do not lie
or know of cruel guile.

And when the youthful days are gone
we keep the precious dreams,
that once belonged to young hearts
that forever are entwined.

Victoria Bern

CHALK AND CHEESE

We're as different as chalk and cheese.
She likes always going out -
whilst I prefer to be at home.
Loud heavy music gives her pleasure,
but it's the classics that I treasure.

We're as different as chalk and cheese.
I like things quite neat and tidy -
whilst she just throws things everywhere.
She likes movies that make her cry,
teases me saying my books are dry.

We're as different as chalk and cheese.
She likes parties all through the night -
whilst with regret I'm the first to leave.
Cliff top walks and salty air filled haze,
following behind she drifts in a daze.

We're as different as chalk and cheese.
Candle-lit meals for me are great -
whilst take-aways suit her best.
The angels smiling down from above,
laugh at the differences that make our love.

B Webster

MISSING YOU

Missing you is much more than not having you near.
When I don't hear from you it's like being deaf,
for nothing sounds as good as that chirping 'Hi'.
When you're not near the world's an empty place,
for I feel alone, adrift in a void, waiting till
I find an island, it's when next I see you.
When I don't see you, it's like being blind, for
nothing is beautiful when you're not around to make
it shine.

So what's missing you?
It's hurting when you're not near, worrying when
you're late, being saddened by your worries and
your tears, missing those beaming smiles, wanting
to know that you're okay, and that you'll make it
through the day.
It's missing you with all my heart, my very soul, so
much so that I'm out of control.
It's being adrift and alone without your warmth.

Osamah Gahin

MY VALENTINE

I love you, woman on the bus,
This card is just to say,
I don't even know your name
But I love you anyway.

You always stand there at the front
In your pretty sheepskin coat.
Yesterday you had a cough,
I've taped on a sweet for your throat.

If you would like more from me
Than just a lemon Zube,
Maybe you could ask me out
While we're waiting for the tube.

If you've got a boyfriend
Or you're married already,
Just say nothing and suck the Zube
And I'll know that you're happy.

Malcolm Lisle

LET YOUR HEART BE YOUR GUIDE

Do not seek perfection in a changing world,
    Instead perfect your love.
    If you have a troubled heart,
    Act out the words above.

Let your mind become clear like a still forest pool,
    open your heart and see.
    If you find nothing there,
    It was not meant to be.

If this isn't what you want to hear,
    Don't look full of sorrow.
    Only now can we truly love,
    So take a look tomorrow.

Every life has a measure of sorrow,
    Sometimes to this we awake.
    If you cannot find your love,
    Then love's not the path to take.

Remember these words when your feeling down,
    And anger shall have no part.
    It has a lot to do with justice,
    But strength is the product of a steady heart.

Sarah Griffin (14)

SWEET DREAMS

I wish I had a sweetheart
That loved me through each day
Of one that I could be a part
And who took my cares away
One to walk along beside
The green fields and the rivers
That flow in with the tide
With cold that gives the shivers
The nature of the woodland
With birds singing above
When walking hand in hand
Would be a sign of love
The trees would whisper
The leaves would sway
But the sun would shine
For us, on that happy day.

Barbara Bevan

SEASHELLS

You and me
        two seashells stranded
                on a shore of sofa
        sandy hue.
Me and you
        devoid of the life
                we once contained.
        The grit of disappointment
        now ingrained
longing for the
        cathartic ocean.
                Nose-diving to the
        blue swirly carpet.

Raine Simmons

LOVE IS

Love is walking down the lane
hand in hand and not seeing
the flowers.

Love is kissing each other
with our two lips meeting
without mistletoe.

Love is two bodies bonded together
in a loving embrace
without chains.

Love is getting married and promising
to look after one another
for evermore.

Love is having our children and
watching them grow up into
nice people.

Love is growing old together and
seeing our grandchildren
playing.

Love is still being in love
now that we're senior citizens.

That is really what
love is.

David Brownley

JULIE, I LOVE YOU VERY TRULY!

Julie, I love you very truly, yeah!
Truly, you do mean so much to me, yeah!
I'll love you till the day I die.
Then in Heaven when I'm in the sky, Oh yeah!
Julie, I love you this is very true.
I love you, yes I really do.

Julie, I love you very truly, yeah!
Truly, you are someone special to me, yeah!
I hate it when we say goodbye.
When you leave me, well I always sigh, Oh yeah!
Now I always want to thank you,
For being such a true friend of mine.

I love you, there's no other.
I love you, hear me say.
I love you, like no other.
I love you, you make my day.

Julie, I love you very truly, yeah!
Truly, my emotion is running through me, yeah!
I love you with all my heart.
Through every day from the very start, Oh yeah!
How I always want to thank you,
For being such a true friend of mine.

I love you, every second.
I love you, and I can say.
I love you, more than can be reckoned.
I love you, in every way.

Julie, I love you very truly, yeah!
Truly, you are very special to me, yeah!
I love you and I hope you see.
You are the only girl for me, Oh yeah!
Julie, I love you this is very true.
I love you, yes I really do.
Julie! Yeah!

Graham Mitchell

THOUGHTS ON THE MARRIAGE OF AN ONLY SON

You came to me in water and blood one sizzling night in July,
A startled peach baby, who smiled in his sleep, too merry to cry.
Years passed; the flaxen boy, soon fatherless and brotherless, grew tall,
Capricious, infuriating, loving, a bright magnet for all.
Now, on a cold day in May, with blossom confetti in the air,
You wait in a music-drenched, flower-incensed church for your
                              bride sweet and fair,
Too far away for me to touch, but near enough for you to smile.
A fanfare: Victoria enters with calm grace the floral aisle,
Veiled in frothy tulle, like mist over an ivory silk cascade,
Trailed by statuesque sisters, sculpted in slub cinnamon brocade.
Ghosts throng the church, delicate, ephemeral, valedictory -
Your long-dead father, infant brother, ancestors through history,
Crowding like stars, joining prayers with ours, a benevolent conclave,
Blessing you both, for they know life and love survive beyond
                              the grave,
Symbolised by the eternal circles of precious rings exchanged,
As two interlocked families are now forever rearranged.
No priest ever asks a mother, 'Who gives this man?' If he were to,
I would answer, 'I gave him life; I now gladly give him to you,
Dearest daughter-in-law.' For, above the trivia, stands your vow,
And Peter's too: that God is love, that love is yours, that love is now.

Chantal Voas

SUCH A TINY WORD

Love is such a tiny word,
And yet it says so much.
It's the utter joy a mother feels,
With her new baby's touch.
It's the hand that reaches out with care,
Another's pain and hurt to share.
It's looking through a child's eyes,
In wonderment at star filled skies.
And being held by someone dear,
When in our eyes we have a tear.
It's being on a sun-kissed hill,
Having the time to stand quite still.
To be with friends and share a meal.
The hug, given with love, that heals.
It really is a little thing,
Without which, life would lose its zing!

Jennie Schofield

NEED YOUR LOVE

I need to see your loving face
Helps set my mind in place
I need to hold your caring hand
My heart beats like a brass-band
I need to kiss your gentle lips
Sends shivers down spine to toe-tips
I need to feel safe in your love
It's my idea of Heaven above

Constance Moss

SO PURE WITH GRACE

So pure with grace,
and fair of face.
Soft like satin, pretty as lace.
Is it really love, in this case?

Happiness, they say, is with a brace
(that's a couple, two, of course) and love being the base;
Like glittering diamonds on the Royal mace;
Like perfumed flowers in a painted vase,
tho' life and love now, such a tragic waste . . .

. . . and the world mourns, lost now, the race,
the peace process, it seems, died within its pace.
Where feelings of men and children's lives adjace-
ent to the real needs, leaving such a bitter taste -
for love is of the asking, blown to the winds, lost, in space(?)
the tracks of tears still looming, or, just in case . . .
fighting not desisted, wipe away the entire race,
futility abound now when love should've taken its place . . .

. . . that's all we needed, so make haste
if thy will, before life we know becomes so hard, to trace;
Reneged on life and nature have we, more interest in oil and Versace

when all we needed - was love
to end the gore and bloodied taste
that threatens life on Earth's dear old face;
Her heart is gone, her soul's to waste
as we think, of course, only, the finery and lace . . .

goodbye to all of that, my friend,
all, we need is love to defer the end . . .

Ron Matthews Jr

NOTHING MORE

I care not for you now. Yet, when you speak,
My eyes rest on your lips, see nothing more.
I care not for you now. Yet still I seek
A shadow of the love that passed before.

(Before, when you were all - all I believed,
Before, when no new ground could shake my trust,
Before, when I - bereft - your absence grieved,
And grieving, bade my future turn to dust).

I care not for you now. So, if it seems
My silence in your presence equals awe,
Be told then: you are constant in my dreams -
And that, for this, I care not. Nothing more.

Julie Martin

IAN

I feel your gentle touch on my back,
as you say goodbye.
That is enough to know
you
are with me
when you close the door,
and I am alone.
If you know the going will be tough
a special hug to help me
on my way
tells me all I need to know
someone cares and is thinking
of me
until we meet again.

Angela Patchett

SEVEN DAYS WITH APRIL

Our dates were like formal meetings
Your heart wasn't there
Just the silky smile you laddered
Speaking through the chair.
I slowly read the minutes
From the melancholic clock,
And when your resignation came, it came as no great shock.

When 'Yes' you'd breathed seven days before,
My heart had leapt the roof,
But my vertigo showed
At the height of my youth.
Your eyes and lips seemed evidence
You truly shared my goal
But the smile that you wear sheer hides a seventy denier soul.

Your eyes that I would die for
Hanging from your face
Your dreams that I would kill for -
In which I had no place
Your lies that I would stand for
That you might give them rest.
I found out when you spoke the truth, I liked your lies the best.

Can I call myself 'ex-boyfriend'?
Allow me, please, that much -
To fabricate a woman's heart
I never really touched.
I apologise for the seven days
I cast you as my bride.
I'm now wed to my apology - it's always at my side.

Keith Edghill

SAY IT WITH FLOWERS

Love is like a rose bud
The petals will unfold
To send a perfumed message
Sweethearts can behold.

Love is like a lily
A pure and precious gift
When feeling down or lonely
'Twill give the heart a lift

Love is in a bride's bouquet
Held with pride and care
Hoping for a perfect life
For the happy pair.

Flowers say a lot to us
Convey a love so true
When sick, a tender nosegay
Will send health shining through

When you need to send your love
A bunch of flowers will do
And in a very little while
You'll find a love that's true

V Tank

TRUE LOVE

Love is very special
So treasure it with care.
If you have found real true love
Nothing with it can compare.

Love forgives and love forgets.
No malice does it bear.
It's kind and oh so patient
Its tenderness to share.

Neglect it at your peril
It will dim, then fade away.
This love that was so precious
You'll regret it went that way.

So hold fast to your true love.
This precious gift so rare.
Nourish it and cherish it
To keep it always there.

Joan Tolhurst

DEATH OF AN EX-PARTNER

They told me yesterday that you had died
And since that news I've known no peace at all
The jumpy cinematograph of passing time
Reels back to moments and occasions I recall

When we communicated easily with our eyes,
Told plans of our intentions with our lips,
No spoken word was needed, no big give away,
We planned the next love-making with our fingertips.

Your even, pretty teeth, when I could focus close,
Bring floods of tears to me as I remember
There was a training course; each day I slipped away.
Our girls were both at school. It was September.

That inappropriate kiss hard on my mouth,
It left me staggering around for days.
Your body signals indicated something new.
I was unsure what message they conveyed.

But we looked forward still to nights,
But always afterwards it was just a game.
The state of truce and equalness with other partners was for me
(I've never ceased to love you) never quite the same.

John Hollyer

THAT SPRING BY THE ANCIENT SEA

Those were the golden hours, Honey,
    Rainbow coloured and deep rose-red,
Sunshades and sandalled feet
    And lazy days by the shores of the Med.

Wine-hazy, piazza evenings,
    With Georgio strumming his song;
Low lights and a 'cool' guitar
    And you and me humming along:

We were 'la musica' then, Caro,
    We dwelt in a flower-scented dream,
Tuscan talk ran amok on our tongues
    And Love was our only theme.

Those were the glowing hours, Dearest,
    When the sea-moon shimmered at night
And we swam through blue-silken water -
    Oh, how our hearts were light,

Light as swansdown, Sweetheart,
    That spring by the ancient sea
Where lovers from Carthage and Rome
    Were once spellbound as you and me.

Fragile, ethereal hours,
    Too ephemeral to last,
Drifting away in the summer
    And lost in the mists of our past.

We were clinging to shadows then, Honey,
    Withholding a truth we daren't tell
When deep in our hearts we already knew
    It was time to whisper 'Farewell.'

Dorothy Thompson

MOTHER

There's a very special lady
Who's always there for you,
With all the wisdom of her years
For you she's shed a million tears,
A broken heart, suffered many a time,
For every pain you've gone through,
Her heart has cried in silence, along with you.
Perish the thought for you to know,
How she's prayed for your troubles to go,
And when you're really happy,
with your heart so full of pride,
For have no doubt she will know,
Just by glancing in your eyes,
Should you bring this very special lady
Glory, fame, or even shame, because it's you
   Her love remains unchanged.

Valerie Fairbrass

LOVE HAS A PRICE

Love has a price, a debt to pay
emotions squeezing like a vice
when fickle hearts meet on the way
   love has a price.
The longing time cannot suffice
when lovers act as in a play
goodbyes become like rolling dice
as one must leave, and one must stay
while sunshine fails to melt the ice
the burning soul will find the way
   love has a price.

Andy Petrie

THE USELESS DAY

Lord God I got mad this morning
Not a very good thing to do.
I shouted at my neighbour,
And she'd just got over flu.
Perhaps she didn't mean to shake her mats
Out in the yard, near my open door.
Dust flew inside, grit settled on the floor.
Bread and pies were cooling on the table.
It covered the cakes and jam.
All day I felt quite cross
I shouldn't but I am.

After this I shooed away some sparrows,
But they just came back again.
They were looking for the crumbs,
And then a heavy shower of rain.
My washing was soaked through,
I washed the kitchen floor.
A friend came in, 'Wipe your feet!
Leave your wellies by the door.'
The kids were late, they'd had a fight,
They're going to bed at six tonight
I've been impatient all day, no time for joy.
No thought for others' sorrow.
I've had no place for other folks, but
Lord I'll try harder again tomorrow.

Joan Scher

THE CARNAL DANCE

Take my hand - come dance with me,
Jig the pulsing night away.
The tunes of love are throbbing free;
Let them hold you in their sway.
The beat grasps all in its pounding trance,
And we all join together in the carnal dance.

Twirl me close and hold me near,
Guide me through each tender set.
Feel the music drown your fear -
Are you under love's spell yet?
Multitudes sway in soft, tuned romance,
And we all join together in the carnal dance.

There's the Youthful, and the Needful,
And the Can't-Say-No,
Paired by Wisened, and by Hands-Full,
And by Don't-Let-Go.
See the Vulture, and the Victim,
And the Tender-Loving-Care
Stalking Lamb-Like, seeking Lived-In,
Clutching Soul-Laid-Bare.

Now as the tune begins to fade,
Just spin me one more time,
Before the dying note is played
And lyrics lose their rhyme.
As the music started, we thought we had a chance,
Yet all are cast asunder by the cruel carnal dance.

Viki Lane

SILENT LOVE

My days of working are now done.
No more part-time jobs for me!
I look ahead to lots of fun
In which my talents can roam free!

With Mary always at my side,
With ready smile, ne're e're a frown,
You never know how high I'll ride -
You cannot keep a good man down!

For happy am I with her near;
My days flow by in sheer content.
I now know neither stress or fear -
I am a very lucky gent!

And though I write with tongue in cheek,
As clear my idle scribble shows,
In one sure thing I am not weak -
My love for her still grows and grows!

Though words of love I speak are rare,
For childhood lessons linger long,
It doesn't mean I do not care -
My love for her is deep and strong.

So let the world know here and now,
My love is ever sweet and true,
And to my loved one here I vow -
My Mary, dear, I do love you!

Reg Hunter

PUPPY LOVE

Floppy eared, soaking wet,
Unforeseeable pain, abandoned pet,
Wanted once, but unwanted too,
Homeless yet unloved by few.

Floppy eared, boney ribs,
A life of truth, yet full of fibs,
Born once, lived twice,
Due to an impossible price.

Floppy eared, bare skin,
Never thought it could be so thin,
Eaten plenty, fed none,
And life has not even begun!

Floppy eared, brought for ten pound,
A big price to pay for such a small hound,
Large price, small pup,
A life of chance, that's out of luck.

Floppy eared, no name,
Suffered far too much pain,
Barked once, kicked twice,
Only him will pay the price!

Floppy eared, found a bed,
Now loved and always fed,
Cared for once, got a name,
Puppy love's alive again!

Karen Waite (15)

THE FLOWER AND ME

I pull them off, one by one,
To leave them there, alone, for fun.
I sit and look, all content,
And notice that the stem has bent.
It makes me think and it makes me wonder,
What has caused me to make this blunder.
I know deep down on why I did it,
It's the way, to nature, I throw a hit.
I see a gem that catches my eye,
And wonder how people pass it by.
A one that's small and as pretty as that,
No-one sees, but if I looked like that;
People would look and people would stare.
I'd never be short of people to care.

A dream, for me, is to be that flower,
To hold that intense, creative power.
To have people stop and smell my nectar,
To know my petals are their own little sectors.
To marvel at my amazing beauty,
To wither and die, as my only duty.

Judith Russell

BIRTHDAY LADY

Birthday Lady, lying there,
(Closèd eye and tousl'd hair,)
In the bed she shares with me
In our married unity.

Birthday Lady, walking tall,
(Beauty hers exceeds them all,)
As she makes her graceful way
Proudly through her Special Day.

Birthday Lady sits content,
(Work all done and time well-spent,)
Reading, writing, and the rest;
Loving, caring; she's the best.

Birthday Lady drift away
Into dreams at close of day.
Lying, walking, sits content;
She's *my* Lady - Heaven sent.

Frank L Appleyard

SOUVENIRS OF LOVE

There's not much left to keep in memory's box
Just a few letters, and some golden locks.
But I still hear your funny little laugh.
See, in a silver frame, your photograph.
There's little more, but one bright summer's day,
And a sweet bouquet, which does not fade away.
Its scent will haunt me, in my reverie
As will that special way you looked at me.
Which seemed to mean more, even, than a kiss.
Yes, there remain the little things, like this.
Not much to last me, through the lonely years
Yet, they are still my precious souvenirs.
There's that romantic song we called 'Our tune'
A handful of silver, left by the moon.
The gold of the sun, shining in your hair.
And all the wondrous hours we used to share.
I gave you my heart, and threw away the key,
But you will linger, in my memory.
There must be just one other little thing,
Oh yes, my darling, it's a diamond ring.
But I can't bear to look at that, it's true.
The sight might break my aching heart, in two.

Pauline Ransley

CUPIDITY

What is love what is love?
Do we really know
Is it a tingling in your spine
Or Cupid with his bow?
What is love what is love?
A quick beat of the heart
Is it a great togetherness
Or Cupid with his dart?
What is love what is love?
Does it make you all aglow
Bring a spring into your step
Or is it Cupid's arrow
What is love what is love?
Does it set your mind aflame
Is it something that you want so much
Or is it Cupid's deadly aim
What is love what is love?
Yearning for what you've not
Tenderness and peace of mind
Or is it Cupid's perfect shot
Love is life and love is peace
Happy nights and sunfilled days
Love is almost everywhere
But Cupid gets the praise

Dennis Malin

ONLY YESTERDAY

It seemed like only yesterday, when you really cared
All those memorable together times that once we truly shared
Talking on the phone for hours, walking hand in hand
Nowadays the long silences, I just don't understand

Losing love along the way, no more hesitation
Love has died along with the art of conversation
Those happy memories cherished, that once we dearly had
Love's gone forever and a day, regrettable but sad.

Rita Humphrey

WITH ALL MY HEART

Come close dear love and feel my heart
That beateth but for thee,
No sighs, or fears, just sweet content
Whilst ever near to me.
Come close dear love and closer still
'Til thou and I are one,
For now I have within my grasp
The moon, the stars, the sun.
Come close dear love stay not apart
From this thy lover's touch,
There shall be all sorrows past
When loving means so much.
Come close dear love so let me find
Thy gentlest caress
To sweep me to the apogee
Desiring doth possess.
And when this heart should beat no more
To break my endless vow,
It then, my love, betrayeth me,
But never, ever thou.

P W Pidgeon

TRUE LOVE NOT RICHES

For over 26 years, I've loved you dear,
Cherishing, and caring for you, holding you near.
My love for you, hasn't changed, in this short span of time,
From the day, you said 'I do' I was happy you were mine.

If I had a choice, to be rich, and fancy free,
Or be poor, and happily wed to thee.
I'd choose the latter, this I would wish,
With your love, I don't need money, to feel rich.

The happiness of being married, all these years to you,
Mean far more than riches, after all these years, I still truly,
                                        deeply, love you!
From a young married couple, all those years ago,
To Grandparents, in the future Great Grandparents, you never know.

All you can be sure of, in the troubled times of today,
Is that my love for you grows stronger, every single day!

Ian S Gamble

FIRST LOVE

The first time that I saw you
It was love at first sight
It felt strange, but wonderful
I knew that I was right

We got to know each other
And soon our love grew
Now after a lifetime together
I'm still deeply in love with you.

Joan Williams

LOST LOVE

Jennie my sweet Jennie
I think of you today
And the first time that I saw you
With women making hay
Your curls were all escaping
Around your lovely face
Those dancing eyes and dimples
Beneath your cap of lace
I knew there'd be no other
Upon this earth for me
And thought of us together
Until eternity
But my father had position
I was made to understand
That we were of the gentry
While you worked on the land
He spoke of a betrothal
And how I'd look a cad
I wish I hadn't listened
But I was just a lad
What can I say about my life
Except it's all been false
What cared I for handsome clothes
Or of the latest waltz
You're all I ever wanted
Sweet Jennie if you care
Please wait for me in Heaven
For we'll be equal there.

Maureen Tooze

DYING LAUGH

In life I had to have the last laugh,
For oh god didn't I have to graft!
I held onto you all at my expense,
You only pushed me away at great lengths.
Love and compassion was never there,
When I was ill none of you could care!

When I was dying you wanted me to live,
Sorry world I had nothing left to give!
So you expected something when I'd gone.
My laugh is you were so terribly wrong!
If you can't give when someone's alive,
That's why you have nothing, feel deprived?

Now you think I'm a bitch, that's good,
For at long last you've understood.
The heartache and suffering have gone,
At last I have found where I belong.
God bless you all, I always cared,
Even though you never shared!

Penelope Ann

LOVE HEARTS

Love has no colour,
It comes from within,
It doesn't matter, what skin your living in,
Love is shown in so many ways,
A kiss, a hug, or giving of a bouquet.

It is, what you say or do,
That brings people closer to you.
Happiness, laughter, time spent together,
Just being there for one another.

Men, women, children too,
All need love from me and you,
Open up your hearts and let love in,
Feel the warmth that lies within.

D Tong

FORTIES GIRL

Will you be a forties girl, fifty years from now,
will you dance in an evening dress,
and curtsey as I bow.

And could I have your number, so I know where you are,
and with consent I'd call for you,
in a chauffeur driven car.

And can we dine by candlelight,
In a time that's meant for us,
where waiters serve from golden trays,
creating such a fuss.

And when we're dancing, on the floor,
the lights will start to fade,
and out will come the guitar man,
and you he'll serenade.

And I'll give you the finest things,
you'll drink the best champagne,
but from this my only wish,
your heart is what I'd gain.

So will you be my forties girl,
fifty years from now,
and will you dance,
in an evening dress,
and curtsey as I bow.

Trevor Wiggan

CARLA, CHAMELEON

Time and foolish time again,
I fell for rough, dark, ruthless men.
Then Ischia - out of the blue
And golden seascape, behold, *you!*
Viking blonde, a teasing smile.
'Can I sit with you a while?'

The day burned on, the sun turned red.
'Come, Carla, swim with me.' You said.
Merman and maid, we plunged together.
Then, a sudden change of weather.
A cruel wind blew across the Quay.
'Carla, please - come home with me.'

We sped to your lair in a sleek, silver car,
And you gave me a book you'd found in a Bazaar.
A transfixing tale of a man for a boy,
Of erotic obsession, of pain. Of pure joy.

You read me some passages, vivid and wild
And I found myself starting to cry, like a child.
And then, gently, you taught me how to unfold
Beneath you, and gradually I grew more bold.

Mentally changing my feminine gender,
As you tenderly taught me new ways to surrender.
Now I'm Carla, chameleon, free from all fear.
With my body I worship you, my dearest dear.

Elizabeth Mark

LOVE

Oh, Love,
why do you treat me so,
when I need to sparkle
like the sun on the water?
When I long to soar
like the seagull,
from the waves
to the sky above.
Oh, Love,
why do you desert me so,
melting away
as the falling snow?

Hopes and dreams
are all frustrations,
Lovers as trains
just leaving stations.
Always the travels
but no destinations!

As a fire-fly
on a summer's night,
I yearn my heart
will soon take flight.
Setting my world aglow
so bright;
I will at last feel
love is right.

Oh, Love, awake me,
one sweet morn.
With a gentle kiss
when comes the dawn.

Freda Ball

WORDS

P	is for the pointless suffering you endure,
A	is for the anguish that we all feel so pure,
I	is for ignorance the ones that don't want to know,
N	for the nonsense said because pain does not show.
H	is for the hope you get from family and friends,
E	is for emptiness felt when experts say it depends,
L	is for the love from people close to you,
P	for the pointless struggle of days you go through.
L	is for the living that you know must go on,
O	is for the others that give hope when all is gone,
V	for versatility you must have from day to day,
E	for everyone who give love, names I need not say,
W	for the woman at my side through my strife,
I	for the incidents we go through together in life,
F	is for the forgiveness she shows with her heart,
E	is for ever and ever, our love shall never part.

A Ferguson

MY HEART IS YOURS

I never thought that I could feel this way,
And now I look forward to each new day,
A love like this, I never thought that I would find,
My love for you is so strong,
You are always on my mind.

As I lay down to go to sleep,
My prayer to God is your love I will keep,
I fill with pride when I walk at your side,
My love for you I just can't hide,
It lights my eyes and shines deep from within.

My heart is yours forever more,
And all my love I give to you and that's for sure,
For now I know that my life has started anew,
Darling, it's your love that makes me feel the way that I do,
My future love and happiness I will always share with you,
And I intend to spend each waking hour just loving you.

Terri Brant

WHAT SYMBOLISES LOVE?

As a child one's greatest love, is found within a toy
maybe a doll with a little girl and a teddy with a boy
something to share all those precious moments . . . of -
sadness and grief, comfort and love.

Then follows the teen years of lascivious drooling
as the idol of your dreams is on stage, there crooning
your heart exploding from the passions of your emotions
as you conjured up idyllic lovesweet notions.

From sweethearts to lovers . . . then wedded bliss
nothing on earth could've been sweeter than this
but then there was the cute puppy or adorable cat
who'd smother you with affection, no doubt about that.

Dorothy J Meddings-Ellis

A FLOWER

I saw a flower I had never seen before
With its beauty and charm I craved for more
Standing alone so full of grace
Shining like a beacon upon my face

Caring for that flower I did so well
Until under its aura I had fell
Tending it with care each day
A special chemistry, who can say

Then a cruel twist of fate from my grasp did steal
For the flower didn't know just how I feel
When it pierced me with its thorns unjust
I brushed it aside as I felt I must

I abandoned that flower, thought the pain would go
I fooled myself, how could I know
That I needed that flower as all could see
But it no longer shines like it did for me

I pray it may shine again one day
The flower I passed along the way
To leave a flower not yet in bloom
Must surely cast a spell of doom

Yes it only takes one step to care
For something special that we share
Just one kind word will make it right
And I'll see again that flower shine bright.

James Dow

THE SAFETY VALVE

Love it comes in many forms
For the ways it needs to go
Like love that comes with friendship
That gives a warming glow

Like the love with understanding
Of the many things we do
So with all our different aims
It's there to help us through

Like love for nature or a pet
Or making something fine
Love is there to lend a hand
A pleasure all the time

For love is really precious
That surely can entwine
Two hearts as if just one
That gives life then a shine

Like love that comes with motherhood
Giving out a bloom
So together with her offspring
She's always there in tune

For love can come at anytime
Even when apart
Just like any safety valve
A treasure in your heart

Olive Walters

IT NEEDS BUT LOVE

It needs but love to make hollyberries shine
Against ice blue sky, more vivid than wine.
It needs but love to make snowdrifts seem
Like white waves in an enchanted dream.
It needs but love to turn the frosted sedge
Into a diamond girdle round the water's edge.
It needs but love for my eager heart to glow
With sudden fire, like sunrise on snow.
It needs but love to kindle a dying ember.
But you do not love me. Bleak is December.

Geraldine Page

GRANDMOTHER'S HANDS

Grandmother's hands were old hands,
age speckled, brown and thin,
the bird-brittle bones a frail framework
for her tissue paper skin.
But when teenage tornadoes stormily blew
through the quicksands of my heart,
and I trod through life's marshlands of misery
and the monsoons of tears would start,
her touch dried my tears just as surely
as the sun dries the rain from above,
for what her loving touch taught,
above everything else
was that 'All you need is love'.

Jessica Heafield

INFORMATION

We hope you have enjoyed reading this book - and that you will continue to enjoy it in the coming years.

If you like reading and writing poetry drop us a line, or give us a call, and we'll send you a free information pack.

Write to :-
Anchor Books Information
1-2 Wainman Road
Woodston
Peterborough
PE2 7BU
(01733) 230761